mus
Vancouver

Aerial view of Vancouver / © City of Vancouver

MICHELIN

mustsees **Vancouver**

Editorial Director	Cynthia Clayton Ochterbeck
Editorial Manager	Brent Hannon
Contributing Writer	Brent Hannon
Production Manager	Natasha G. George
Cartography	Peter Wrenn
Photo Researcher	Sean Sachon
Layout	Sean Sachon
Additional Layout	Natasha G. George
Cover & Interior Design	Chris Bell, cbdesign
Cover Design & Layout	Natasha G. George

Contact Us

Michelin Travel and Lifestyle North America
One Parkway South
Greenville, SC 29615, USA
travel.lifestyle@us.michelin.com
www.michelintravel.com

Michelin Travel Partner
Hannay House
39 Clarendon Road
Watford, Herts WD17 1JA, UK
www.ViaMichelin.com
travelpubsales@uk.michelin.com

Special Sales

For information regarding bulk sales, customized
editions and premium sales, please contact us at:
travel.lifestyle@us.michelin.com
www.michelintravel.com

Michelin Travel Partner
Société par actions simplifiées au capital de 11 288 880 EUR
27 cours de l'Ile Seguin - 92100 Boulogne Billancourt (France)
R.C.S. Nanterre 433 677 721

MIX
Paper from
responsible sources
FSC® C015829

Note to the reader:
While every effort is made to ensure that all information printed in this guide is correct
and up-to-date, Michelin Travel Partner accepts no liability for any direct, indirect or
consequential losses howsoever caused so far as such can be excluded by law. Admission
prices listed for sights in this guide are for a single adult, unless otherwise specified.

Butchart Gardens (Japanese Garden in Autumn) p 92

© Courtesy of The Butchart Gardens

Vancouver Aquarium (Strait of Georgia exhibit) p 114

© Meighan Makarchuk / Vancouver Aquarium

Victoria (Inner Harbour) p 86

© Brent Hannon / Michelin

STAR ATTRACTIONS

★★★ ATTRACTIONS

Unmissable historic, cultural and natural sights

For more than 75 years people have used Michelin stars to take the guesswork out of travel. Our star-rating system helps you make the best decision on where to go, what to do, and what to see.

★★★	Unmissable
★★	Worth a trip
★	Worth a detour
No star	Recommended

MUST KNOW

🚗 ACTIVITIES

Unmissable activities, entertainment, restaurants and hotels

Vancouver's awesome setting and abundant opportunities for recreation enliven city life to the nth degree. We recommend every activity in this guide, but the Michelin Man logo highlights our top picks.

🚗 Outings

🚗 Hotels

🚗 Shows

🚗 Relax

🚗 Restaurants

🚗 Shopping

🚗 Side Trips

🚗 Sports

STAR ATTRACTIONS

IDEAS AND TOURS

Throughout this thematic guide you will find inspiration for many different ways to experience Vancouver and its surroundings. The following is a selection of places and activities from the guide to help start you off. The sights in bold are found in the index.

Fishing and Hunting

In British Columbia fishing ranges from **deep-sea** pursuit of salmon and halibut to back country **fly-fishing** for wilderness trout. Key species are chinook, coho, sockeye and pink salmon, as well as rainbow and cutthroat trout. Some fishing excursions are available from **Vancouver★★★** and **Victoria★★★**, most of which are day or half-day trips, but wilderness expeditions are popular, and often use these major cities as their base. Overnight stays at ranches and wilderness lodges with fishing facilities are possible. **BC Fishing Guides** *(604-576-7768 or 1-866-443-FISH; www.bcfishingguides.com)* offers accommodation options, and guided trips on the Fraser River and elsewhere in BC. Nonresidents must obtain a licence, available from sporting-goods stores. For information on seasons, and catch and possession limits, visit www.envgov.bc.ca/fw/wildlife or www.env.gov.bc.ca/fw/fish. For information on hunting trips in BC, and license fees, as well as listings of outfitters, contact the **Guide Outfitters Association of BC** at www.goabc.org.

Golf

Because of its climate, southern British Columbia offers one of the longest seasons for golfing in Canada. Vancouver's **Fraserview, Langara** and **McCleery** golf courses as well as putting greens in Stanley Park and Queen Elizabeth Park are run by the city parks and recreation office *(vancouver.ca/parks-recreation-culture/golf-courses-pitch-and-putts-and-driving-ranges.aspx)*

In **Whistler★★★** world-class courses *(www.golfwhistler.com)* such as **Château Whistler Golf Club, Nicklaus North** and **Whistler Golf Club** were designed by top-notch golfers. Some greens afford ocean and mountain views, and many facilities feature local cuisine and wines. To locate golf facilities in Vancouver and on Vancouver Island, visit www.britishcolumbiagolf.org.

Hiking and Walking

BC has thousands of miles of hiking trails, ranging from urban paths skirting the Vancouver waterfront to wilderness routes that take weeks to traverse. The **West Coast Trail** is a legendary week-long trek along the southwest shores of Vancouver Island that traverses deep forests, sandy beaches, and rocky headlands amid temperamental weather; it is part of **Pacific Rim National Park★★★** *(www.pc.gc.ca)*. Less taxing, but almost as spectacular, is the **Juan de Fuca Trail** to the south.

In Vancouver proper, walking is a pleasure, be it through the varied topography and features of **Stanley Park★★★** or along the

MUST KNOW

Skiing at Grouse Mountain

newer seawall that connected various facilities for the 2010 Vancouver Olympics. **Lighthouse Park★★** on the North Shore has several trails to the lighthouse, and is a great place to see the sun set. Despite its size, Vancouver is a city made for walkers; downtown neighbourhoods are condensed and historic sites abound. Walking tours can be done solo with the aid of a good map, or as guided group expeditions to landmarks of the past.

International Travel Maps & Books (*www.itmb.ca*) offers a large range of maps at its Richmond store. Mountain Equipment Co-op, Canada's REI, has an extensive selection of maps at its stores (*www.mec.ca*).

Bicycling

Vancouver is one of the most bicycle-friendly cities in North America, and the city has actively encouraged cycling by building bike lanes that connect the city in all directions and cross all the major bridges, and by supplying abundant bicycle parking, complete with air pumps. Cycling the Stanley Park Seawall is an immensely popular pastime, while more ambitious cyclists can cycle past English Bay, along False Creek, and eventually out to the beaches of Kitsilano—all on a dedicated bike path. See www.vancouver.ca/bikevancouver for maps and information, while bikes can be rented at Spokes Bicycle Rentals (*604-668-5141; www.spokesbicyclerentals.com*), and Cycle BC (*866-380-2453; vancouver.cyclebc.ca*). Maps and guided tours are also available at Cycle BC.

Skiing and Boarding

With a dozen major destination resorts—and three ski areas just outside Vancouver—British Columbia is a North American ski capital that compares to Colorado. Onshore Pacific weather flows bring dependable snowfall, often in large amounts. Along Vancouver's North Shore, not far from downtown, **Mount Seymour, Grouse Mountain★** and **Cypress Mountain★** offer skiers ready access and prodigious snowfalls *(Nov-Mar)*. All three alpine ski areas offer lighted skiing at night,

Kayaks, False Creek

although only two of them, Cypress and Grouse Mountain, have snow-making equipment. Cypress is the biggest and steepest of the three North Shore ski areas, and is widely regarded as the best. In the run-up to the 2010 Winter Olympics, during which it hosted freestyle skiing and snowboarding events, Cypress added a new high-speed chair lift, a day lodge, and 40ha/98-acres of additional terrain.

World-famous, **Whistler★★★** is often the top-ranked ski resort on earth by ski magazines; its slopes and venues were home to many of the events in the 2010 Vancouver Olympics. Its mountain-base village offers world-class lodging for more than 10,000 visitors, and its two vast mountains constitute the biggest single skiing complex on the continent. Skiing begins at Whistler each year in early November and winds up in June; this long season enables skiers to hit the slopes on a brisk May morning, and tee off at a golf course that afternoon. For a complete rundown on BC ski resorts, visit *www.hellobc.com*.

Water Sports

British Columbia has some of the world's best-known water sports locales, including canoeing and kayaking in and around Vancouver and Victoria. Mountain rivers and lakes provide ideal spots in the wilderness around Whistler, too. Because BC has such a lengthy coastline, and a mixture of ocean and inland waterways, the options are virtually limitless.

Saltwater **Desolation Sound**, north of Vancouver, and **Barkley Sound**, south of Ucluelet on the west coast of Vancouver Island, are famed worldwide among sea kayakers. Both comprise innumerable islands and coves to explore, with hidden sand beaches and, in Desolation Sound, unusually warm waters in late summer.

If your passion is the freedom and intimacy of kayaking, be sure to visit **Clayoquot Sound** and Broughton Archipelago, while Barkley Sound is part of Pacific Rim National Park; for information visit www.pc.gc.ca. Canoes and kayaks are available for rent at many points, ranging from downtown Vancouver at **English Bay** to the Inner harbour at Victoria (visit www.vancouverisland.com/kayaking for more information). Experience the rush of **white-water** kayaking on the buoyant rivers of Vancouver Island. For trip planning and information, visit www.paddlecanada.com.

Wildlife Watching

Visitors to the province regularly see bears, beavers, deer, moose, caribou and other woodland fauna; as well as whales, bald eagles, seals, sea lions and numerous other shore creatures. Such wildlife is not abundant on downtown Vancouver streets, obviously, but skunks, raccoons, coyotes, and even bears are sometimes encountered in city-based locales such as **Stanley Park**. Wildlife-watching adventures depart from Vancouver and Victoria, by road or by water, to take camera buffs and nature lovers on day-long outings within short range of these major cities. The northern section of **Georgia**

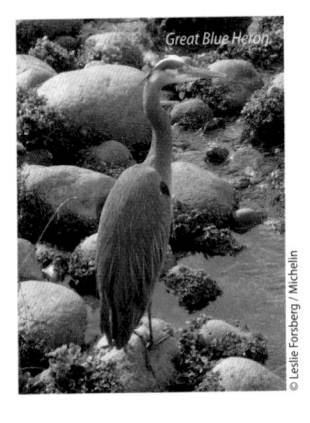

Great Blue Heron

© Leslie Forsberg / Michelin

Strait is renowned for its whale-watching, though controversy is growing over the practice, which can disturb the whales. For information about Canadian wildlife, visit the **Canadian Wildlife Federation** website: www.cwf-fcf.org or call them at 800-563-9453, and **Environment Canada's** website at www.ec.gc.ca. Wildlife is best observed in BC's provincial and national parks, although thousands of visitors are astounded to discover bears, moose, elk and other large animals simply browsing the roadside vegetation along highways in the interior and on Vancouver Island. When watching or photographing wildlife, a respectful distance is crucial. It is illegal, and dangerous, to interact with wild animals in any way, especially by feeding them. Wildlife advocates argue that any human action that causes wild animals to change their behaviour is wrong. Stiff fines are given in parks for feeding and otherwise habituating wildlife; in any case, large animals such as bears and moose can be quite hazardous.

Farms and Markets

A large swath of the land around urban centres in BC hosts farms. In fact, the **Okanagan Valley★★** and rural areas around Vancouver form the western branch of Canada's three main "bread baskets," together with the Niagara Peninsula, centrally located in Ontario, and the Annapolis Valley of Nova Scotia on the east coast. BC farmers commonly sell their fresh, and sometimes organic, produce, dairy products and meats through collective farm markets or directly from their farms. Not only

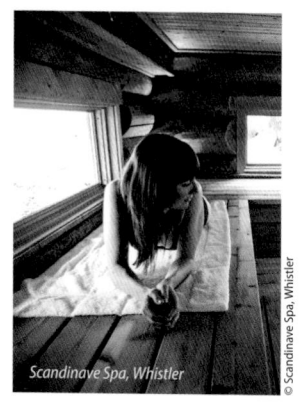
Scandinave Spa, Whistler
© Scandinave Spa, Whistler

does a farm market tour remind participants of where food comes from (hint: not the supermarket), but it results in a cache of delicious edibles for the trip home.

Visit the **Fraser Valley**, Okanagan Valley and **Vancouver Island** for farms abundant with the good things in life, a tasty way to be educated and entertained. Find more information and a farm tour plan by visiting www.circlefarmtour.com. Note: most farms and farm markets sell on a seasonal basis. Visit www.hellobc.

com for more information. If you can't manage to get out of town for a few hours or a day, let the farmers come to you; Vancouver and Victoria both have excellent city-based farmers' markets, the best of which is year-round on **Granville Island★★**; visit www.granvilleisland.com for details.

Spas
See Spas.

The spa retreat has become a popular getaway vacation in Vancouver, Victoria and Whistler. Some of Vancouver's long-established beauty/therapeutic and medical spas helped create the Canadian spa industry, and continue to expand its horizons by incorporating new treatments based on locally available herbs and other botanicals, as well as treatments entrenched in native practice.

Most major urban hotels incorporate day spas among their facilities; fees vary according to the treatments requested. Many are located in Vancouver or Victoria proper or within an hour's

Entrance to Mission Hill Family Estate winery
© Brain Sprout / Mission Hill Family Estate

drive from each; both cities are resplendent with day spas. Spa retreats are found in sublime non-urban locales, typically set amid spectacular scenery, and are often included as part of larger resorts such as ranches or wilderness lodges.

Echo Valley Ranch and Spa *(800-253-8831; www.evranch.com)* lies 435km/270mi northeast of Vancouver via Whistler or Fraser Canyon routes. Overnight guests choose from a variety of Asian spa treatments at the full-service spa. For a list of BC destination spas, visit www.hellobc.com.

Wineries

See BC Wine Country and Cowichan Valley. With about 200 wineries—many within an hour or two by car from Vancouver—this area has become a major and well-recognized New World wine region. From big-output winery production facilities to small family-run vineyards with limited vintages, the choices are vast and varied. The combination of diverse, award-winning wines, stunning scenery and the laid-back sensibility of BC wine regions makes for a pleasurable day of sampling. To ensure you don't mix sipping and driving, local operators offer guided tours in buses. Visit www.hellobc.com for more information, or to participate in an **Okanagan Valley★★** winery tour, visit www.okwinetours. com. A great way to enjoy winery expeditions is to tour the vineyards during the day and find a perfect restaurant in the city for dinner that night, one with a wine list that focuses on local vintages.

Quick Trips

Stuck for ideas? Try these:

IDEAS AND TOURS

CALENDAR OF EVENTS

Listed below are the most popular events in the Vancouver area, including Vancouver Island. Dates are subject to change. For the most current information, contact **Tourism Vancouver** (*604-682-2222; www.tourismvancouver.com*); **Tourism Victoria** (*250-953-2033; www.tourismvictoria.com*); or **Tourism BC** (*800-435-5622; www.hellobc.com*).

January

Chinese New Year Festival
604-681-1923, Chinatown, www.cbavancouver.ca
In Vancouver, the Chinese Benevolent Association celebrates with a colourful parade to toast the arrival of the new year in late January or early February. Some 50,000 people watch marching bands, dancers, martial artists and floats, accompanied by smoking, blazing firecrackers.

Vancouver International Boat Show
604-678-8820, BC Place and Granville Island, www.vancouverboatshow.ca
Now expanded to include an in-water venue (the marina at Granville Island), the show is designed to awe and inform, with new boats on display, new products to make boating and

February: Vancouver International Wine Festival

© Vancouver International Wine Festival

sailing safer, and seminars that help experienced and novice sailors get into the groove. There are even boat rides to inspire future sailors.

February

BC Home & Garden Show
604-639-2288, BC Place Stadium, www.bchomeandgardenshow.com
This show offers hands-on fun for every aspect of home life, including HGTV stars who take to the stage for witty talks on making the most of your domicile.

Vancouver International Wine Festival
604-872-6623, Vancouver Convention Centre, www.vanwinefest.ca
Almost 800 wines from some 200 wineries in nearly 20 countries. Attendees enjoy tastings, wine dinners and wine seminars in venues throughout the city; book early, as many events sell out.

February: BC Home & Garden Show

© Reformation PR / BC Home & Garden Show

March

Pacific Rim Whale Festival
250-726-7798, Tofino, Ucluelet,
www.pacificrimwhalefestival.com
The focus is watching gray whales,
but events include the annual Gala
Dinner and Silent Auction at the
Wickaninnish Inn.

Vancouver International
Dance Festival
604-662-7441, Various venues,
www.vidf.ca
VIDF offers everything from
classical ballet to interpretative
performances by individuals and
troupes. Adjuncts include an art
exhibit and dance workshops.

April

Vancouver Sun Run 10k
604-689-9441, Downtown.
www.vancouversun.com/sunrun
This 10km road race is not
technically a charity run, but it
has donated millions to amateur
athletics and national literacy.
In 2011, 60,000 participants made
it the largest event of its kind in
the world.

May Swiftsure
International Yacht Race

© Janice Hayward / Swiftsure International Yacht Race

World Ski & Snowboard
Festival
604-938-3399, Whistler,
www.wssf.com
This winter-sports event has
fashion shows, outdoor concerts, a
film and photography showdown,
a "silent" disco (dance to music
delivered through headphones),
and a dog parade.

May

Swiftsure International
Yacht Race
250-592-9098, Victoria Inner
Harbour, www.swiftsure.org
This prestigious yacht race, hosted
by the Royal Victoria Yacht Club, is
for sailors with the experience to
negotiate the rugged coastline of
the Juan de Fuca Strait. The event
holds three long overnight races,
and a shorter single-day course.

Vancouver International
Children's Festival
See For Kids.

April Vancouver Sun Run

THE VANCOUVER SUN RUN

© Ric Ernst / Vancouver Sun

Dragon Boat Festival

© Photo by Jeremy Dyson / Dragon Boat Festival

June

Bard on the Beach
See Performing Arts.
BC Shellfish and Seafood Festival
250-890-7561, Comox,
www.bcshellfishfestival.ca
Enter the oyster-shucking contest or chowder challenge, or watch a shellfish cooking demonstration at this 10-day event. Booths offer wares from hand-crafted jewellery to produce.
Dragon Boat Festival
604-688-2382, False Creek,
www.dragonboatbc.ca
This popular summer event mixes thunderous drums, team spirit, high-energy boat racing, and music. Teams of dragon boats are put together, often within the corporate culture and mostly with a charitable undercurrent.
Vancouver International Jazz Festival
See Performing Arts.
Vancouver Storytelling Festival
604-876-2272, Various venues,
www.vancouverstorytelling.org
Held every other year.
This festival was founded by Vancouver area librarians, and it emphasizes the traditional art of old fashioned story-telling. While there are numerous adjuncts to the festival, the sharing of stories is the magical focus.

July

Canada Day (July 1)
604-665-9000, Canada Place and Granville Island,
www.canadaday.canadaplace.ca
www.granvilleisland.com
Paint your face white and maple-leaf red and dance all day, then watch fireworks at night as Canada celebrates another year.
Celebration of Light
See Performing Arts.
Theatre under the Stars
See Performing Arts.
Vancouver Folk Music Festival
See Performing Arts.
Vancouver Pride Week
604-687-0955, Various venues,
www.vancouverpride.ca
The Gay Pride parade is the highlight of Pride Week, and rainbows abound as the LGBT community takes to the streets. Thousands of spectators watch as the parade winds its way through the West End.

August

Pacific National Exhibition
604-253-2311, Hastings Park (through Sept), www.pne.ca
The "PNE" opened in 1910 and has since established itself as one of North America's top annual fairs. With midway rides and games, live music, exhibits, seminars, horse and dog shows, and contests for the best in produce and livestock, it's a circus of fun at the end of summer.

September

Vancouver Fringe Festival
See Performing Arts.

**Vancouver International
Film Festival**
See Performing Arts.

October

**Vancouver International
Writers & Readers Festival**
*604-681-6330, Granville Island,
www.writersfest.bc.ca*
Tributes to literary greats, readings
by authors, and a celebration of
ideas and written creativity mark
this festival, a favourite of great
Canadian writers (Alistair MacLeod,
Jane Urquhart and Margaret
Atwood, for example) and
their fans.

Haunted Village
*604-297-4565, Burnaby Village
Museum, www.burnabyvillage
museum.ca*
Stroll through five ominous-
looking haunted buildings in
Deer Lake Park and the Burnaby
Village Museum, a spooky event
that takes place in the dark of
the night, and includes trick-or-
treating, Halloween entertainment,
ghostly costumes, and rides on the
museum's antique carousel.

December: **Festival of Lights**

© Raymond Chan / Photomedia / VanDusen Botanical Garden

Vancouver Fashion Week
*778-996-2200,
www.vanfashionweek.com*
Fashion designers from around
the world and across the street
merge during this week, showing
everything from haute couture
to streetwear, and everything in
between. The focus is on local
designers, but this event has
become one of the most vital
international fashion events on the
Pacific Rim. It has changed venues
over the years; see the website for
the latest details.

December

Festival of Lights
*604-257-8335,
VanDusen Botanical Garden,
www.vandusengarden.org*
Every branch, bloom and blade
is decked out in lights at this
glittering annual celebration, and
hundreds of thousands of lights
in all colours sparkle in the dark
as visitors stroll down Candy Cane
Lane. Throughout the gardens
can be heard the sweet sound of
Christmas carols, and kids can visit
with Santa Claus and his elves.

October: **Haunted Village**

© Burnaby Village Museum & Carousel

CALENDAR OF EVENTS

19

PRACTICAL INFORMATION

WHEN TO GO

The main **tourist season** for most of Canada, including Vancouver and all of British Columbia, begins the last weekend in May (Victoria Day) through the first weekend in September (Labour Day). Travel is especially heavy in July and August. Many attractions extend the season to the Thanksgiving weekend (second Monday in October), though tourist crowds diminish considerably after Labour Day. From early April to mid-May, visitors can usually enjoy comfortable daytime temperatures but expect cool nights and light showers in the **spring**. July, August and September are ideal for outdoor activities such as sailing, kayaking, canoeing or hiking. Warm, sunny days with temperatures ranging from 22°–25°C/70°–80°F characterize the **summer** months. Oddly enough, though it is surrounded by water, Vancouver experiences little humid weather in the summer. October can be the best month to visit, since sunny days are not uncommon, and the deciduous trees put on a bright display. For the sports enthusiast, **winter**, generally from mid-November to mid-March, offers excellent opportunities to enjoy downhill skiing, cross-country skiing, dogsledding, snowshoeing and snowmobiling. All these activities are possible both on Vancouver Island and on the mainland, most notably in Whistler (*see Excursions*).

KNOW BEFORE YOU GO

Before you go, contact the following organizations in and around Vancouver for information about sightseeing, accommodations, recreation and annual events.

Tourist Offices

Tourism Vancouver

www.tourismvancouver.com – 201-200 Burrard St., Vancouver, BC V6C 3L6 Canada. 604-683-2000.

Tourism BC

www.hellobc.com – British Columbia Visitor Centre @ Peace Arch, 298 Highway 99, Surrey, BC V3S 9N7 Canada, 604-541-4555 or 800-HELLO-BC.

Tourism Victoria

www.tourismvictoria.com – 812 Wharf St., Victoria, BC V8W 1T3 Canada. 250-953-2033 or 800-663-3883.

Tourism Whistler

www.whistler.com – 4010 Whistler Way, Whistler, BC V0N 1B4 Canada. 604-932-3928 or 800-944-7853.

Average Seasonal Temperatures in Vancouver				
	Jan	Apr	Jul	Oct
Avg. High	6°C/43°F	13°C/55°F	22°C/72°F	14°C/57°F
Avg. Low	1°C/34°F	5°C/41°F	13°C/55°F	7°C/44°F

Visitor Centres

Tourism Vancouver
200 Burrard St., Plaza Level, Vancouver.
Open year-round daily 8:30am–6pm.

Tourism Victoria
812 Wharf St., Victoria.
Open May–Sep daily 8:30am–8:30pm. Rest of the year daily 9am–5pm. Closed Dec. 25.

Tourism Whistler
4230 Gateway Dr., Whistler.
Open year-round daily 8am–10pm.

Useful Websites

In addition to the official tourism websites above, try these sites for useful visitor information:

www.canada.com – Provides local, regional and national features on all things Canadian.

www.canoe.ca – The website of a media provider offering news, movie listings, sports, weather.

www.cbc.ca – Canadian Broadcasting Corp. website for news, sports and entertainment.

www.pc.gc.ca – Parks Canada lists all of the country's national parks, historic sites and areas, and takes reservations.

www.vancouversun.com – The city's leading daily newspaper, which provides extensive coverage of arts, entertainment and sports in Vancouver.

www.canada.com/the province – The *Vancouver Province* is a tabloid that offers a down-to-earth perspective on local affairs.

www.straight.com – The Georgia Straight, the city's alternative weekly, has comprehensive arts and entertainment coverage every Wednesday.

www.cityfood.com – City Food is a monthly devoted to restaurant news and reviews.

www.dailyxtra.com – *Xtra West*, a free weekly, covers the city's LGBT scene.

www.weatheroffice.gc.ca – Area weather forecasts from Environment Canada.

INTERNATIONAL VISITORS

In addition to local tourism offices, visitors may obtain information from the nearest Canadian embassy or consulate in their country of residence. Embassies of other countries are located in Canada's capital, Ottawa. Many foreign countries also maintain consulates in Vancouver. For further information on all Canadian embassies and consulates abroad, contact the website of the Canadian Department of Foreign Affairs and International Trade: www.dfait-maeci.gc.ca.

Entry Requirements

Travellers from the US need a valid (machine readable) **passport** to visit Canada and return to the US by air. Canadian and US citizens must present a passport to cross the Canada/US border by land or sea. Requirements can and do change; visit www.cbp.gov for the latest information.

21

To bring children into Canada, single parents (whether divorced or simply unaccompanied by their spouse) travelling with children must bring a permission letter from the other parent, as well as a passport or special enhanced ID. Only a **passport** or other appropriate secure document will be accepted for anyone, including US citizens, to enter the US. Check the websites www.canada.travel or www.travel.state.gov (US government site) for the most recent updates. All other visitors to Canada must have a valid passport and in some cases, a visa (see list of countries at www.cic.gc.ca/english/visit/visas.asp). No vaccinations are necessary. For entry into Canada via the US, all persons or legal residents are required to present a valid passport or special US-issued border-crossing ID. Check with the Canadian embassy or consulate in your home country about entry regulations and proper travel documents.

Persons seeking entry to Canada who have ever been convicted of a crime (including marijuana possession) or, in some cases, have ever been arrested, should be aware that they may be denied entry. If you have any doubt, check with Canadian border authorities before heading to Canada.

Border Crossings

For entry into Canada via the US, all persons are required to present a valid **passport** or special government-issued enhanced ID designed for border crossing purposes. The US-Canada border crossing at Blaine is the busiest west of Michigan. Lines can grow long on weekends and holidays; the best time to cross, either way, is early morning weekdays and Sundays. It is usually easier heading north into Canada, which often has more lanes open for border inspection. When crossing the border, do not try to carry contraband. Don't take any weapons into Canada, or Cuban cigars into the States.

Canada Customs

Visitors over 19 years of age entering British Columbia (age 18 in some Canadian provinces) may bring 1.14 litres of liquor or 1.5 litres of wine or 24 cans of beer (totaling a maximum of 8.5 litres) without paying duty or taxes. Tobacco is limited to 200 cigarettes, 50 cigars or cigarillos, 200 tobacco sticks, or 200 grams/7oz of loose manufactured product. Gifts totalling $60 Canadian may be brought in duty-free. All prescription drugs should be clearly labeled and for personal use only; it's best to carry a copy of the prescription. For details, call the Border Information Service (800-467-9999, Vancouver) or write to Border Services Agency, Ottawa, Ontario, K1A 0L5 Canada (800-461-9999; www.cbsa-asfc.gc.ca). Canada has stringent legislation on firearms—do not bring any weapons to the border. For further information on entry of firearms, contact the Canadian Centre for Firearms (284 Wellington St., Ottawa, Ontario K1A 0H8 Canada; 800-731-4000; www.rcmp-grc.gc.ca/cfp-pcaf).

Driving in Canada
See Getting There, By Car, below.

GETTING THERE
By Air
Vancouver International Airport (YVR) is located 10km/7mi south of downtown (604-207-7077; www.yvr.ca). The airport services major domestic and international carriers, with nonstop flights from Asia, Europe and North America. Air Canada (888-247-2262; www.aircanada.com) and its affiliates provide connections to cities throughout the province.

Taxi service to downtown costs $35. Major car rental agencies are located at the airport.

A great way to get to the airport is via the Canada Line **SkyTrain**; it travels from the airport to downtown in 26 minutes (http://tripplanning.translink.ca/).

Airport Fees
Upon departure from some Canadian cities, travellers should be prepared to pay an **Airport Improvement Fee**, though it is usually collected by the airline as part of the ticket price. If not, passengers leaving Vancouver and flying within British Columbia pay $5, and those flying out of the province pay $20.

By Train
Daily service to Pacific Central Station at the east end of downtown (1150 Station St.) is provided by **VIA Rail**. Canada's national passenger service, VIA Rail links major cities within the country. In Canada, consult the telephone directory for the nearest office or call 888-842-7245 or see the website (www.viarail.ca). This station is also the terminal for **Amtrak** service from the US (800-872-7245; www.amtrak.com).

By Bus
Pacific Central Station (1150 Station St.) is Vancouver's departure point for all buses. For travel from the US or within Canada, contact **Greyhound** (604-683-8133 or 800-661-8747; www.greyhound.ca). **Quick Shuttle** (800-665-2122 www.quickcoach.com) offers frequent service from Vancouver to Seattle, and points between.

By Car
Vancouver lies at the westernmost end of the Fraser River Valley in southwestern BC. The main highway access from the east is Highway 1, the Trans-Canada Highway. From the south, access is along Highway 99, which becomes Interstate 5 when it crosses into the US at the Blaine border crossing. Drivers from the US may use enhanced state-issued licences. Visitors from elsewhere should obtain an International Driving Permit through their national automobile association in order to rent a car. Drivers must carry vehicle registration and/or rental contract, and proof of insurance at all times. Gasoline is sold by the litre. Vehicles in Canada are driven on the right-hand side of the road.

Car Rental Companies
+ **Alamo** – 800-233-8749 www.alamo.com.
+ **Avis** – 800-879-2847 www.avis.com.
+ **Budget** – 800-268-8900 www.budget.com.
+ **Dollar** – 800-800-4000 www.dollar.com.
+ **Enterprise**– 800-261-7331 www.enterprise.com.
+ **Hertz** – 800-654-3131 www.hertz.com.

- **National** – 877-222-9058
  www.nationalcar.ca.
- **Thrifty** – 800-847-4398
  www.thrifty.com.

GETTING AROUND
Orientation

Downtown Vancouver sits on a small peninsula bordered by saltwater inlets on both sides, with Stanley Park at the northwest end. Most of Vancouver's downtown city streets are laid out in a **grid pattern,** with streets running southeast-northwest and northeast-southwest.

The main downtown arteries are Granville, Burrard and Denman streets, running northeast to southwest; and Davie and Georgia streets, running southeast to northwest. Georgia Street is the thoroughfare that leads to the Lions Gate Bridge, heading to the North Shore; Granville and Burrard streets cross their namesake bridges over False Creek heading south.

To the southwest, walking and cycle paths run from the beaches of English Bay around False Creek and on to Kitsilano. The West End is largely residential. Yaletown's new residential towers line False Creek. Avoid East Hastings Street area (*see On Foot*).

On Foot

Vancouver is best seen on foot. Most downtown sights can be reached within a half hour (or less) from major hotels; from Stanley Park, at one end of downtown, to Chinatown at the other, is a 30-minute walk. (Do not walk along **East Hastings Street,** from about Gore Ave to Carrall St., a drug district.) Street numbers rise as you go westward and northward; even numbers are on the east or north sides of the street.

By Car

Vancouver's **rush hour** extends from 7:30am–9am, and 4pm–6pm, and is comparable to any other congested North American city. Some streets, such as South Granville, are likely to be crowded any time between 6am and 10pm. **Speed limits**, posted in kilometres, are generally 100km/h (60mph) on freeways, 90km/h (55mph) on the Trans-Canada routes through town, and 80km/h (50mph) on most highways. The speed limit in cities and towns slows to 50km/h (30mph). **Headlights** must be turned on at all times. The use of seat belts is mandatory. Parking spaces on downtown streets are limited, and parking regulations are strictly enforced. Limited metered parking is available on non-arterial streets, and parking lots and garages are plentiful. Posted rush-hour restrictions generally prohibit parking and stopping 7am–9am and 4:30pm–6pm (times vary). For up-to-date road conditions, see www.drivebc.ca.

Parking

Parking signs are colour-coded: green-and-white signs indicate hours when parking is allowed; red-and-white signs indicate hours when parking is not allowed. Stopping during restricted times could result in your vehicle being towed. Parking spaces identified with a handicapped symbol are reserved for people with disabilities.

Traffic on Burrard Street Bridge

© City of Vancouver

By Public Transportation

TransLink *(604-953-3333; www.translink.bc.ca)* operates an extensive system of public buses, ferries **(SeaBus)** and light rail lines (**SkyTrain**, **West Coast Express**) in Vancouver. Hours of operation are: Mon–Sat 6am–1:30am, Sun 9am–1:30am. Adult fares one-way range from $2.75–$5.50 (exact fare required; drivers do not sell tickets). A **Day Pass**, good for unlimited one-day travel, is $9.75. Transfers are free between buses, public ferries and light rail. System maps and timetables are available free of charge.

By Taxi

Numerous taxi companies operate in the city under municipal licensing supervision—drivers must demonstrate knowledge of English, be courteous and prove their familiarity with the city. When the "Taxi" sign on the roof of the cab is lit, the vehicle is available for hire. Most downtown runs cost $10-$15 (on average $1.92/km); from downtown to the airport costs about $35. Vancouver's major taxi companies include **Yellow Cab** (604-681-1111) and **Black Top Cabs** (604-731-1111). **McLure's Cabs** have been serving Vancouver since 1911 (604-831-1111).

By Ferry
See below.

GETTING TO VANCOUVER ISLAND AND VICTORIA

Even though Highway 1 starts in Victoria (and goes all the way to the island of Newfoundland), you can't just drive to Victoria—the Strait of Georgia intervenes. That's why thousands of people hop in their vehicles on Friday afternoons to get in line for ferry passage to Vancouver Island. The bad news is, there are thousands of island-hoppers; the good news is, advance planning and flexibility will allow you to bypass the worst of the crush.

By Ferry

BC Ferries, the province's ferry service, operates three runs to the island from the Vancouver area (888-223-3779; www.bcferries.com).

The Tsawwassen terminal south of the city (follow Granville St. south to Hwy. 99) serves ferries crossing to both Swartz Bay (Victoria) and Duke Point (Nanaimo and the rest of the island).

The Horseshoe Bay terminal in West Vancouver (at the continental end of Hwy. 1, take Georgia St. west across the Lions Gate Bridge) serves ferries to Nanaimo, as well as other destinations. All three runs to the island consist of large boats departing roughly every two hours. Once you reach the island, it's about a half-hour drive into downtown **Victoria** from Swartz Bay; and three hours from Nanaimo to Tofino. Passage for a vehicle and driver varies by season and day, but peaks at about $70. To beat the crowds, make an advance reservation. The ferries' reserved boarding service carries a premium—$22, or $15 if booked seven days in advance— but it's worth it.

By Air

Several airline operations fly between Vancouver and the island. The two most popular airlines both depart from downtown sites near Canada Place.

Helijet (800-665-4354; www.helijet.com) flies Bell Jet Ranger craft to a landing pad at the entrance to Victoria's inner harbour. Passage takes about 25 minutes; the view of the Gulf Islands is wonderful.

Harbour Air (departs from downtown floatplane base just west of Canada Place; 800-665-0212; www.harbourair.com) flies floatplanes—mostly the de Havilland Beavers and Otters that are considered some of the sturdiest planes ever built. Passage to Victoria takes about 40 minutes.

ACCESSIBILITY

Most public buildings, public transit and ferries, and many attractions, restaurants and

BC Ferries

© BC Ferries

MUST KNOW

hotels in Vancouver provide **wheelchair access**. Disabled parking is provided and the law is strictly enforced. For details, contact Tourism Vancouver. Many national and provincial parks have restrooms and other facilities for the disabled (such as wheelchair-accessible nature trails or tour buses). For details about a specific park, call 888-773-8888 or check online at www.pc.gc.ca. Passengers who need special assistance with train travel should contact VIA Rail Special Needs Services (888-842-7245 or 800-268-9503/TDD; www.viarail.ca). For information about bus travel, contact **Greyhound Canada** (800-397-7870/TDD; www.greyhound.ca).

Additional information is available from the BC Office for Disability Issues (250-356-5991 or 250-387-3114/TDD); or from the We're Accessible Quarterly (to request a copy, call 604-576-5075).

ACCOMMODATIONS

For a selection of places to stay overnight, see Hotels at the back of the guide.

Reservations Services

Tourism Vancouver – 604-683-2000; www.tourismvancouver.com.
Tourism BC – 250-387-1642 or 800-663-6000; www.hellobc.com.
British Columbia Bed & Breakfast Innkeepers Guild – www.bcsbestbnbs.com.
BBCanada – www.bbcanada.com

Major hotel and motel chains have locations in Vancouver:

- **Best Western** – 800-780-7234 www.bestwestern.com.
- **Choice Hotels** – 877-424-6423 www.choicehotels.com.
- **Days Inn** – 800-225-3297 www.daysinn.com.
- **Delta Hotels** – 888-890-3222 www.deltahotels.com.
- **Fairmont** – 800-257-7544 www.fairmont.com.
- **Four Seasons** – 800-819-5053 www.fourseasons.com.
- **Hilton** – 800-445-8667 www.hilton.com.
- **Holiday Inn** – 877-660-8550 www.holidayinn.com.
- **Marriott** – 888-236-2427 www.marriott.com.
- **Radisson Inn** – 800-333-3333 www.radisson.com.
- **Ramada Inn** – 800-854-9517 www.ramada.com.
- **Sheraton** – 800-325-3535 www.starwoodhotels.com/sheraton.
- **Westin** – 800-937-8461 www.starwoodhotels.com/westin.

Campgrounds
BC Parks: 800-689-9025; www.env.gov.bc.ca/bcparks

Hostels
There are three large hostels in Vancouver, two downtown and one at Jericho Beach (*see Hotels*). Many other destinations in BC have hostels; contact Hostelling International-Canada (800-663-5777 or www.hihostels.ca) for other hostels in the province.

COMMUNICATIONS

To call long distance within Canada and to the US from landline phones, dial 1+ **area code** + number. For overseas calls, dial 011, or refer to the country codes in most telephone directories, or dial "0" for operator assistance. Many operators in Canada speak English and French. Collect calls and credit card calls can be made from public pay phones, which are becoming increasingly rare.

For local directory assistance, check the white pages of the phone directory or dial 411 (fee may apply); outside the local area code, dial 1+ area code + 555-1212. Telephone numbers that start with **800, 866, 877** or **888** are toll-free (no charge) to North American phone service customers, though some European phones cannot utilize these toll-free numbers. A local call costs 50 cents. Be aware that many hotels place a surcharge on all calls.

Area Codes

Throughout British Columbia, you must dial the **area code** plus the seven-digit number to make a local phone call. Before you leave, check with your home carrier to ensure your **cell phone** will operate in Canada. Area codes for Vancouver and the Lower Mainland, including Whistler, are 604 and 778. For the rest of British Columbia, including Victoria and Vancouver Island, the codes are 250 and 778.

Cell/Mobile Phones

Cell (mobile) phone coverage is widespread in and around British Columbia's cities, towns and popular tourist attractions but remains sketchy or nonexistent in remote areas of the province. Coverage varies with different carriers, but most phones have full service in cities and towns. Some cell phones whose providers cover most of North America do not require the initial '1' for long distance; users simply dial the applicable 10-digit number to reach phones anywhere in Canada and the US.

Emergency Numbers

911 service, operated through municipalities, is extensive in British Columbia, and can be accessed from cell phones; if for some reason 911 doesn't work, dial "0" for the operator and ask for the police.

Internet Access

High-speed Internet service (Wi-Fi) is available in virtually all hotels in Vancouver, Whistler and on Vancouver Island, as well as in

Important Phone Numbers	
Emergency (police, ambulance, fire department, 24hrs)	✆911
Police (non-emergency)	✆604-717-3535
Crime Stoppers	✆800-222-8477
24-hour Pharmacy Shoppers Drug Mart, 1125 Davie Street	✆604-669-2424
Weather	✆604-664-9010
Road Conditions	✆800-550-4997
Canadian Automobile Association	✆604-268-5500

Measurement Equivalents										
Degrees Fahrenheit	95°	86°	77°	68°	59°	50°	41°	32°	23°	14°
Degrees Celsius	35°	30°	25°	20°	15°	10°	5°	0°	-5°	-10°

1 inch = 2.54 centimetres (cm)
1 mile = 1.6 kilometres (km)
1 quart = 0.94 litres
1 foot = 30.48 centimetres (cm)

1 ounce = 28 grams (gm)
1 pound = 0.45 kilograms (kg)
1 gallon = 3.78 litres

many restaurants and coffee shops. Some visitor centres also provide Internet access.

BASIC INFORMATION
Discounts
Prices in this guide are shown for a single adult only, unless otherwise stated. Discounts may be available for the following:
Senior Citizens – Many attractions, hotels, restaurants, entertainment venues and public transportation systems offer discounts to visitors age 62 or older (proof of age may be required). Canada's national parks usually offer discount fees for seniors. For more information, contact the Canadian Association of Retired Persons (888-363-2279; www.carp. ca). Visiting seniors should feel free to ask specific businesses if a discount is available. **Students** – Discounted prices might be available for students with proof of student status. Be sure to ask.

Electricity
Voltage in Canada is 120 volts AC, 60 Hz. Foreign-made appliances may need AC adapters (available at specialty travel and electronics stores) and North American two-prong, flat-blade plugs.

Mail/Post
Post offices across Canada are generally open Monday to Friday 8am–5:30pm; extended hours are available in some locations. Sample rates for first-class mail (letter or postcard; up to 30 grams): within Canada 85 cents; to the US $1.20; international mail $2.50. Note that rates typically rise every year, in January. **"P" stamps** do not show a value and can be used indefinitely once they are purchased. Mail service for all but local deliveries is by air. For information regarding postal codes or locations of facilities, visit www.canadapost.ca.

Metric System
Canada has largely adopted the International System of weights and measures. Weather **temperatures** are given in Celsius (°C), and fluids are usually sold by millilitres and litres, though grocery items are often sold, confusingly, in both metric and imperial units. All distances and **speed limits** are posted in kilometres (to obtain the approximate equivalent in miles, multiply by 0.6). *See chart above.*

Money

Canadian Currency – Canada's currency is based on the **decimal system** (100 cents to the dollar). Bills are issued in $5, $10, $20, $50, and $100 denominations; coins are minted in 5 cents, 10 cents, 25 cents, $1 and $2; pennies are no longer in circulation. The Canadian dollar fluctuates with international exchange rates, usually within 10 percent of the value of the US dollar. All prices shown in this guide are in Canadian dollars unless otherwise specified.

Credit/Debit Cards – You don't need to carry much cash while visiting Canada: ATM machines are widely available, and most merchants accept debit or credit cards. Self-serve gas stations, parking lots and grocery store check-outs are common vendors where credit and debit cards are accepted. Do carry a few "loonies" or "toonies" (the $1 and $2 coins) for parking meters, tips and snacks. Most public telephones accept calling cards at no charge, but local calls cost 50 cents (two quarters). To report a lost or stolen credit card: American Express (800-668-2639); Diners Club (866-890-9552); MasterCard (800-307-7309); or Visa (800-847-2911).

Currency Exchange – Exchange money at banks for a favourable **exchange rate**. The most favourable rate may be through credit card companies.
Visitors can exchange currency at downtown banks as well as at Vancouver International Airport. Most banks charge a percentage fee for this transaction. Private exchange companies generally charge higher fees. Airports and visitor centres in large cities may have exchange outlets, as do some hotels.

Travellers' Cheques – Some banks, stores, restaurants and hotels accept travellers' cheques with photo identification. However, many merchants today are reluctant to accept traveller's cheques. In addition, Canadian bank systems have converted to the chip-and-pin credit cards used in Europe, but US-style magnetic-stripe cards are still usable at many self-serve pay-points. US travellers are best advised to buy gas at stations with registers manned by clerks who can process a signature purchase, as a precaution.

Opening Hours

Business hours in British Columbia are, for the most part, Monday to Friday 10am–5pm. In general, retail stores are open Monday to Friday 9am–6pm (until 9pm Thursday and Friday), Saturday 9am–5pm, and Sunday noon–5pm, though longer hours are becoming more common. In most cities, shops are open on Sunday afternoon, and small convenience stores in gas stations may be open much later.

Banking institutions are generally open Monday to Friday 9am–5pm; some bank branches are open on Saturday morning, and some offer extended evening hours.

Smoking

British Columbia has one of the toughest anti-smoking laws in North America. Smoking is banned in all public spaces, including restaurants, bars and private clubs, building lobbies and any other enclosed space where people

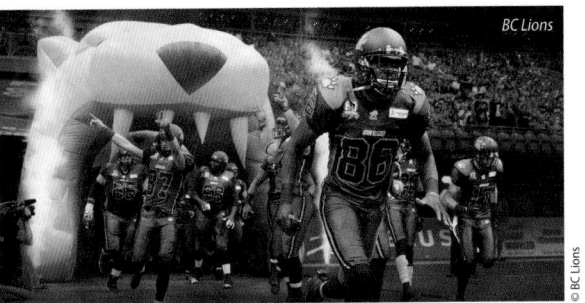

gather. There may be designated smoking rooms in hospitals and health institutions, but otherwise the only public place you can light up is outdoors, and not near (within 3 metres) a door, windows or air intake. Smoking has been banned from aircraft, buses, trains and most offices for some time. Visitors may still smoke in their own hotel rooms; many hotels continue to have smoking floors.

Spectator Sports

Vancouver is a great place to be a spectator at sporting events. The city's major professional sports teams include:

- **Football/BC Lions (Canadian Football League)**
  late June–November
  BC Place
  604-589-7627
  www.bclions.com
- **Hockey/Vancouver Canucks**
  (National Hockey League)
  October–June
  Rogers Arena
  604-899-7444
  http:// canucks.nhl.com
- **Baseball/ Vancouver Canadians**
  (Northwest League of Professional Baseball)
  April–September
  Nat Bailey Stadium
  604-872-5232
  www.canadiansbaseball.com

Taxes

Prices displayed in Canada do not include sales tax.

Vancouver Taxes – The former HST (Harmonized Sales Tax) has returned to a split federal and provincial sales tax, distinct from other provinces in Canada. In British Columbia, the federal portion (Goods and Services Tax or GST) is 5 percent, and the Provincial Sales Tax (PST) is 7 percent, while hotel room taxes in Vancouver add up to 16.5%.

Time Zone

Vancouver is located in the Pacific Standard Time zone (PST), eight hours behind Greenwich Mean Time and three hours behind New York City.

Tipping

It is customary to give a small gift of money—a tip—for services rendered to the following service providers: waiters (15–20 percent of bill), porters ($2 per bag), chambermaids ($1 per day) and taxi drivers (15 percent of fare).

PRACTICAL INFORMATION

PORT OF CALL: VANCOUVER

As the largest port on the west coast of Canada, Vancouver is home to dozens of cruise lines that tour the coast south and north of the city, as well as points on Vancouver Island such as Victoria and Nanaimo.

A Top Destination

Vancouver is a destination for cruise ships as well as a popular port of call for multi-stop cruises that sail the Pacific Northwest and the South Pacific. While Vancouver itself is a huge draw for cruise-ship tourism, it is perhaps best known as being the starting point for ships traveling to **Alaska**. Most major cruise lines offer Alaska cruises from Vancouver, and some include Vancouver in their ports of call for cruises from San Francisco, and points further south.

The ideal Vancouver-based cruise offers the best of the two worlds that the city straddles: beautiful natural scenery and the vibrancy of a world-class city. A combination of coastal cruising and land excursions to spots such as

Whistler, **Fraser Valley** wineries, **Granville Island**, North Vancouver and **Victoria** is a perfect blend. There are, of course, locally operated **small-cruise companies** that take guests on runs through English Bay and Burrard Inlet, among other popular spots within the city and surrounds, but don't go out to sea. Others offer dinner cruises or daytime tours, or can be rented for private parties.

Due to weather restrictions, cruises heading north through the **Inside Passage** and up to Alaska operate from May to September. Many of Alaska's glaciers are still ice-packed in summer, so this is an ideal time to enjoy the luxury of the cruise while marvelling at inlets and fjords and humpback whales.

Lions Gate Bridge and cruise ship

© City of Vancouver

Cruise Lines

A number of cruise lines serve the port of Vancouver, Vancouver Island and Victoria. Below is a selection of the major lines that serve the area.

Celebrity Cruises
www.celebritycruises.com or 1-800-647-2251.
Celebrity offers primarily cruises that depart Vancouver and make the Alaskan coast run, with stops at the **Prince William Sound** glaciers, Brooks Falls at Katmai National Park and **Juneau**, with views of Mount McKinley (weather permitting). This company also sails the more southerly Pacific coastline with Wine Cruises from San Francisco to Vancouver, including stops at Victoria and Nanaimo in British Columbia, and Seattle in Washington State.

Holland America Line
www.hollandamerica.com or 1-877-932-4259.
Holland America delivers shoreline cruises to explore the immediate areas around Vancouver, including the Capilano Suspension Bridge, Chinatown, Gastown and Stanley Park, and **Butchart Gardens** on Vancouver Island. Vancouver is a destination vacation for this cruise line, which also includes Vancouver as a port of call on their multi-port packages.
Holland America offers 24- and 58-day Pacific cruises that stop at Vancouver, as well as exotic locales like Sydney, Australia, Hawaii, Pogo Pogo, Fiji and New Caledonia.
A relaxing long weekend could comprise a three-day cruise that stops at Vancouver, Astoria (Oregon) and San Francisco.

Norwegian Cruise Line
www.ncl.com or 1-866-234-7350.
Norwegian endeavours to give travellers a lot in a compact period, with 7-day cruises that include stops at San Francisco, Los Angeles, Vancouver, Victoria, Nanaimo, and Astoria. They also provide week-long cruises from Vancouver to Alaska. One of the most reasonably priced of the major lines, especially for travellers who book early.

Oceania Cruises
www.oceaniacruises.com or 1-855-623-2642.
A slightly smaller organization that pays particular attention to upscale details, Oceania Cruises start sailing from Vancouver to Alaska and back in mid-May; booking in advance can net as much as a 50 percent discount and optimum luxury while you visit and see the **Inside Passage**, Ketchikan, Juneau, Sitka and Wrangell, with an awe-inspiring pause at Tracy Arm Fjord and Sawyer Glacier.

Princess Cruises
www.princess.com or 1-800-774-6237.
One of the world's favourite cruise lines, Princess has been running the **Vancouver-to-Alaska** route for about four decades and knows what travellers want most. With extended stay options, visitors can spend more or less time in Vancouver as they choose, and can enjoy **add-on excursions** to highlights such as Stanley Park, Robson Street and Granville Island. Most of the Alaska-bound cruises include a visit to Victoria, and focus on the star attractions of Alaska: fjords, glaciers and whales.

PACIFIC RIM PARADISE

Sparkling Vancouver is truly a city of the world. Poised on North America's Pacific Rim—and at the forefront of urban life—this cosmopolitan city boasts a spectacular natural setting, a strong economy, high marks from both residents and visitors, and a level of cultural diversity matched by few other metropolitan areas.

It's all about lifestyle here. Vancouver has it all: a mild climate, fabulous restaurants, world-class hotels, great cultural attractions, recreational opportunities and stunning scenery. It's no wonder that Vancouver has always been rated highly among hundreds of competitors as the "**most liveable city** in the world," ranking third in 2014.

The place now called Vancouver was once just large, lofty trees surrounded by shellfish-laden beaches and salmon-rich waters, and populated by the **First Nations peoples**. Although the waters of British Columbia (BC) were first explored by Spanish seafarers, it was British Royal Navy officer Captain **George Vancouver** who charted the area for Britain in 1793. The first European settlers, trappers and traders established posts for the **Hudson's Bay Company** in the early 1800s. In

1858 the discovery of gold in the BC interior brought global attention to the region, but the real wealth of the coast turned out to be **timber**.

In 1863 the first sawmill was built on Burrard Inlet, and as the towering old-growth Douglas firs and western red-cedars were felled, development sprang up in the clearings. European, Asian and American immigrants flocked to BC in the latter half of the 19C to work in the timber and fishing industries. When the **Canadian Pacific Railway** chose Burrard Inlet as the terminus for its transcontinental rail line in 1885, Vancouver's future was assured. Today Vancouver thrives as Canada's Pacific hub, and the largest port in the country— trade in BC as a whole supports approximately 20 percent of area jobs. **Tourism** has assumed huge significance, with nearly 9 million

---

Fast Facts

- **History:** First European settlement was established in 1863; Vancouver was incorporated in 1886.
- **Population:** 650,000 (city); 2,400,000 (18 Lower Mainland municipalities)
- **Distance to the US border:** 24 miles/38.6km
- **Annual precipitation:** 46 inches/1,168mm
- **Top 10 languages spoken, in order:** English, Punjabi, Cantonese, Mandarin, Tagalog (Filipino), Korean, Persian, Spanish, Hindi, Russian.
- **Mother tongue:** Half of Vancouver's school-age children were raised speaking a language other than English.

Aerial of city including
Canada Place and Burrard Inlet

visitors a year to Vancouver. The city hosts the annual Vancouver International Film Festival, held in the early fall since 1982. The **film industry** spends more than $1.2 billion annually in and around the city. Filmmakers like the fact that BC's diverse landscape means that somewhere within a few hours of Vancouver is a setting that can substitute for almost any place in the world, while the city's famously temperate climate assures virtually nonstop production. That moderate *terroir* also enables BC growers to produce a vast array of fruits, vegetables, herbs and wines that Vancouver chefs utilize, blending continental and Asian influences with Pacific seafood, to create a distinctive regional fare known as **West Coast cuisine**. For the visitor, Vancouver is a remarkably user-friendly city. Although there are no freeways, travel from the airport to downtown takes less than half an hour. Once you're downtown, the vast majority of attractions are within **walking distance**, including Stanley Park, the Art

Gallery, Canada Place, Gastown, Chinatown, and Yaletown. Canadians are helpful and friendly, and the Canadian dollar **exchange rate** has traditionally favoured those spending American dollars, British pounds and euros, though in recent years it has been closer to par with the US dollar. On top of all that, everywhere you look is **spectacular scenery**: glistening blue water, majestic forests, and towering snowcapped mountains. The proximity of these landscapes encourages skiing, golf, hiking, bicycling, boating and other outdoor recreation for residents and visitors alike.

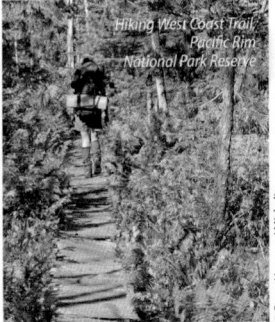

Hiking West Coast Trail,
Pacific Rim
National Park Reserve

PACIFIC RIM PARADISE

NEIGHBOURHOODS

Visitors should allow extra time to explore Vancouver's distinctive neighbourhoods. The vibrant West End is one of the densest residential districts in North America, while Kitsilano is a gentrified former hippie haven that is now a wonderful place for families to live and work. Hip Yaletown borders a massive urban development, Concord Place, that has transformed much of False Creek into a glittering collection of high-rise residences. Chinatown is a fine place for a morning stroll, while Commercial Drive provides Italian flair, open-air markets and affordable dining and nightlife.

CHINATOWN★

Bounded by Keefer, Abbott and Hastings Sts. and Gore Ave. www.virtualvancouver.com/ chinatown.html.

Though Vancouver's Chinatown is small by North American neighbourhood standards, it is big by Chinatown measurements— the **third-largest**, exceeded only by Chinatowns in New York and San Francisco. It dates back almost 150 years, to the days when Chinese labourers were brought across the Pacific Ocean to build the Canadian railroads and wagon roads. Its continuing vitality reflects the mid-1990s exodus from Hong Kong to Canada, as well as Canada's history of welcoming immigrants. To this day, more than half the district's residents list Mandarin or Cantonese as their native language.

It's best to explore Chinatown on foot, so you can take in the sights, sounds, smells and tastes of the dynamic Asian cultural mix; start at Pender and Carrall streets, head east three blocks to Gore, then south a block and back west on Keefer Street. Along the way, the exotic world of **Asian life** flavours every step. Numerous food stalls offer dozens of different Pacific **seafood varieties,** and large tanks of crab and lobster. Other stalls overflow with everything from dried fish and scallops (used for flavouring) to glistening honey-glazed roast quail—which makes a great mid-morning snack. Keep your eyes peeled for jackfruit, an enormous tropical fruit bigger than a watermelon.

Chinatown Classics

Tea is more than simply a beverage to the Chinese, and at **Ten Lee Hong Tea & Ginseng** (*500 Main St. 604-689-7598*) you can experience a formal tea ceremony and investigate the dozens of medicinal uses for ginseng—which would truly be a miracle substance if it accomplished everything its adherents claimed it did. Fans of Chinese cooking won't want to miss **Ming Wo** (*23 E. Pender St. 604-683-7268; www.mingwo.com*), a small warehouse stacked floor-to-ceiling with cookware, including the greatest variety of woks you're ever likely to see. Established in 1917, the store now has four downtown locations, and one each in North Vancouver, Richmond and Burnaby.

MUST SEE

Jade Water Pavilion, Dr. Sun Yat-Sen Classical Chinese Garden

© Dr. Sun Yat-Sen Classical Chinese Garden

The Best of Chinatown

Dr. Sun Yat-Sen Classical Chinese Garden★
578 Carrall St. at Keefer St.
See also Parks and Gardens.
This classical Chinese garden is the district's visitor highlight, but the smaller, less developed **meditation garden** adjacent to it *(toward Quebec St.)* is also lovely in its own right, and there's no admission charge. Both gardens honour the father of modern China, Sun Yat-Sen (1866–1925).

Chinese Benevolent Association
[A] refer to map on inside front cover. 108 E. Pender St.
The association's home (1909) is a lavishly painted example of a tong headquarters—**tongs** being community support associations, not the pseudo-gangs as often supposed.

Chinese Cultural Centre Museum & Archives
555 Columbia St. 604-658-8880. www.cccvan.com. Open Tue–Sun 11am–5pm.
Adjacent to the Sun Yat-Sen garden, the cultural centre was founded in 1973 to foster understanding of the Chinese people and to promote Chinese culture and art. It accomplishes these goals by hosting special events, celebrations and language classes, as well as changing art exhibits.

The centre also houses an evocative **museum** describing the experience of Chinese-Canadians in their new homeland as they faced the struggles common to all immigrants. Upstairs, you'll learn about the impressive record of

Touring Tip

Though Chinatown itself is perfectly safe during the day, the stretch of **Hastings Street** west of the district is an area plagued by drug trafficking and drunkenness, and it's not advisable to walk through it at any time, day or night. To walk to Chinatown from downtown, it's best to take **Pender Street.** The intersection of Main and Hastings streets, in front of the old Carnegie Library, suffers the same problem—tread warily.

NEIGHBOURHOODS

Chinese-Canadians who served in the country's military.

Chinese Freemasons Building
[B] refer to map on inside front cover. 5 W. Pender St., northwest corner of Pender and Carrall Sts.
It is rumoured that Sun Yat-Sen secretly lived in this 1907 structure when he came to Vancouver in the early 20C. Here he plotted with the Chi Kung Tong, a powerful Chinese secret society, to overthrow China's failing Qing Dynasty government.

Sam Kee Building
[C] refer to map on inside front cover. 8 W. Pender St., southwest corner of Pender & Carrall Sts.
At 1.8m/6ft wide, this two-storey building claims to be the world's narrowest office building. A property-line dispute forced the narrow design of the structure. It now houses an insurance agency, and yes, employees work in the building's narrow confines.

Floata Seafood Restaurant
180 Keefer St. 604-602-0368. www.floata.com.
With headquarters in Hong Kong, the largest Chinese restaurant in Canada can seat 1,000 (yes, one thousand) people. Almost every table will be filled on a busy day, so don't arrive late. Specialties include dim sum and Peking duck, which is barbecued on-site.

WEST END★
Bounded by Thurlow St., False Creek and English Bay, Stanley Park and Georgia St.
With high-rise apartments packed cheek-to-jowl along tree-lined streets, the West End is one of the highest-density residential areas in North America. The heart of the neighbourhood is **Denman Street,** a European-style artery lined with small shops, cafes and bistros. Here, fruit and vegetable vendors offer fresh produce from all climes and culinary persuasions, and local independent coffee houses compete with larger national chains like the popular Canadian coffee and donut shop, Tim Hortons.
The West End was the first "suburban" residential development in the young city's life—city fathers prevailed on Cornelius van Horne, the ultra-powerful nabob of the Canadian Pacific Railway, to use his influence in Ottawa to back Vancouver's plea for title to a military reserve—now **Stanley Park**. The park

Chinatown Cuisine: Dim Sum
One of the many translations of this Mandarin term is "little treats," and each serving is indeed small, and a treat. But a meal composed of a half-dozen dim sum baskets is anything but modest—baked, fried or steamed pastries, buns, cakes and dumplings are always filling and often intensely flavoured. Common "packaging" materials include wheat, rice and taro flour; some dim sum arrive wrapped in banana leaves, while some have no wrapping at all, like the chicken feet that fascinate—and repel—most Westerners. Fillings include shrimp, fish, squid and other seafood, pork, chicken, bean paste, tofu, custard and fruit preparations, and many more—more than 500 kinds of dim sum already exist, and new ones are being created all the time.

MUST SEE

Filming Stargate Atlantis

© Creative BC

Set Pieces

Though *The X-Files* brought Vancouver new prominence, the city has long been a film industry magnet—and it remains so, with more than $1 billion in TV and film production a year in BC. There is literally never a day that a production isn't shooting somewhere in or around Vancouver—Stanley Park, the Art Gallery grounds, Gastown and Yaletown are common settings. You are quite likely to encounter a film shoot by chance, but you can refine the process considerably by accessing the **Creative BC** website for a list of current productions and locations (*Creative BC, 2225 West Broadway. 604-736-7997; www.creativebc.com*). Please bear in mind that, among other things, the industry likes Vancouver because city residents believe in practicing simple courtesy with stars: it's fine to watch them, but not to invade their privacy.

made the new West End housing development considerably more attractive. The neighbourhood's transition to mid-rise apartments occurred largely in the period between World War II and 1960.

English Bay Beach★★
Beach Ave. and Denman St.
If you're in Vancouver in the winter, spring or fall months, you may wonder why the beach here looks so neatly tended, the sand raked and logs lined up back from the water. Do people really swim here? Yes, they do. In July, August and early September, English Bay's shallow water warms sufficiently to welcome all but the wimpiest souls. By noon on sunny days, assorted families and sunbathers, with their towels and

picnic baskets, will be spread out by every log. Kayakers paddle by, kids splash in the shallows, and every once in a while, when the wake from a container ship reaches shore, intrepid body surfers hop on a break for a short ride. When you're lying on the beach with the palm gardens (*see Parks and Gardens*) behind you, it's not easy to believe you're in the homeland of ice hockey.

Touring Tip

Take a gelato break morning, noon or night: be sure to stop in at **Milano Coffee & Gelato** (*849 Denman St. 604-681-1500*) to sample the dozens of Italian-style gelati and ices.

NEIGHBOURHOODS

◆ **English Bay Bathhouse** offers showers and a place to change, and it also it rents kayaks and sailboards.

West End Food Options

The **Robson Public Market** (*1610 Robson St.*) is an indoor aggregation of butchers, bakers, delis and produce vendors who sell everything from North European sausages to East Asian rice dishes. Cuisines available to passersby include Korean at **Madangcoul** (*847 Denman St. 604-688-3585*) and **Damso Modern Korean** (*770 Bute St. 604-806-0945*), soothing pork-broth ramen noodles at **Motomachi Shokudo** (*740 Denman St. 604-609-0310*), the neighbourhood's best sushi at

West End Farmers' Market
© City of Vancouver

Miko Sushi (*1335 Robson St. 604-681-0339*), and Japanese tapas, or izakaya, at **Kingyo Izakaya** (*871 Denman St. 604-608-1677*).

Roedde House Museum
1415 Barclay St. See Historic Sites.

YALETOWN★
Bounded by Davie, Homer, Nelson and Cambie Sts., and Pacific Blvd.
Yaletown isn't the only former **warehouse district** given new life by redevelopment, but it's certainly one of the best-known and the most dynamic. What was, just 20 or so years ago, a seldom-visited area dedicated to the business of shipping has been transformed into a bustling commercial district filled with restaurants, galleries and shops.

Long before it was a warehouse district, Yaletown was the edge of a tidal flatland. The curving brick wall in the tiny park at Mainland and Davie streets marks the shoreline of two centuries ago, before dredging and filling converted much of **False Creek** to dry land. That area also formed a portion of the site of the Expo '86 fairgrounds, part of which has been converted into a massive housing complex called **Concord Pacific Place**.

It all happens along two blocks of Hamilton and Mainland streets, between Nelson and Davie streets. Perched above these two streets, behind the loading docks that once served delivery trucks—now turned into patios and a broad promenade—are some of the city's glitziest restaurants, priciest shops and finest salons. The scene on a pleasant evening, when young office workers flock to the area, rivals that of Greenwich Village or Soho in New York City.

Yaletown Sampler

Here are some "musts" among Yaletown's many restaurants and shops:

◆ **Barbara Jo's Books to Cooks** – 1740 West 2nd Ave. 604-688-6755. www.bookstocooks.com.

◆ **Blue Water Cafe + Raw Bar** – 1095 Hamilton St. 604-688-8078. www.bluewatercafe.net.

◆ **Chintz & Company** – 950 Homer St. 604-689-2022. www.chintz.com.

◆ **Cioppino's Mediterranean Grill** – 1133 Hamilton St. 604-688-7466. www.cioppinosyaletown.com.

◆ **Vancouver Cigar Company** – 1093 Hamilton St. 604-685-0445. www.vancouvercigar.com.

COMMERCIAL DRIVE

From E. Broadway to Venables St.
This heart-and-soul neighbourhood – also known as "Little Italy" – is a bastion of authenticity in a city that is undergoing wholesale gentrification. In this former Italian

Roundhouse Community Arts & Recreation Centre

181 Roundhouse Mews, in the Concord Pacific Place development. 604-713-1800; www.roundhouse.ca.

Once upon a time Canadian Pacific engineers used the huge turntable here to juggle locomotives and railcars. The railroad is long gone, but the turntable forms the centrepiece of the courtyard for an intriguing neighbourhood centre. Outside, a massive retired locomotive thrills kids and rail fans, while the gallery space inside features temporary shows by local artists and craftspeople. It's a worthy reminder of this now chic neighbourhood's working-class past.

© City of Vancouver

enclave, ethnic heritage remains visible in its enticing collection of pizza and pasta houses, gelato stands, and Italian groceries and streetside markets. In the wake of Vancouver's property boom, "the Drive" has become an eclectic haven for students, office workers, newcomers from elsewhere in Canada, and other folks who like an urban environment, but can't afford the soaring rents and sky-high restaurant bills that typify the city's more upscale neighbourhoods.

Italian Delights

Commercial Drive's Italian heritage can be sampled at **Federico's Supper Club** (*1728 Commercial Dr., Denman St. 604-251-3473*) where the wonderful pasta dishes are followed by live music and dancing to a rotating selection of bands. An equally fine meal can be had at **Arriva Ristorante Italiano** (*1537 Commercial Dr., 604-251-1177*)

a popular local landmark, while no visit to the Drive would be complete without a cappucino and a sandwich at the semi-legendary **Joe's Cafe** (*1150 Commercial Dr. 604-255-1046*), a well-known neighbourhood fixture.

KITSILANO

Bounded by Burrard St., W. 12th Ave., MacDonald St. and False Creek/English Bay.

"I've got a nice little place in Kits," is the way that thousands of Vancouverites happily explain their residences—and thousands more wish they could. Indeed, thriving, progressive Kitsilano enjoys the best reputation among all Vancouver's residential districts. From 1966 and into the '70s, peace signs were prominent front-door insignias, a VW van was parked on almost every block, and a protest of some sort was the subject of constant telephone-pole posters. Nearby **Vanier Park**

Quintessential Kitsilano

Sophie's Cosmic Cafe
2095 West 4th Ave. 604-732-6810. www.sophiescosmiccafe.com.
With its "garage sale" decor, and a menu that ranges from waffles to falafel to veggie burgers and quesadillas, Sophie's is an institution that has withstood the many tides of change running through Kitsilano. Since it opened in the 1940s, the cafe has specialized in huge breakfast plates, bowls of rich oyster stew, and deep-dish apple pie that towers seven inches high.

Banyen Books & Sound
3608 W. 4th Ave. 604-732-7912. www.banyen.com.
Here you'll find a copy of seemingly every self-help book ever written, as well as a CD inventory that includes flute music from every continent. Founded in the early 1970s, Banyen devotes itself to personal growth in a thoroughly ecumenical fashion—volumes on everything from Buddhist to Zoroastrian thought, and music ranging from Gregorian chants to Paul Winter. Banyen does a thriving business shipping its books and CDs throughout North America.

Monster Homes

Though Shaughnessy itself remains much as it was 75 years ago, the districts on either side of Granville and Oak were the first to experience a phenomenon that has since spread to the rest of Vancouver, in which huge, newly built, box-like houses fill tiny lots that once held much smaller residences. These "monster houses," as long-time Vancouverites call them, were first built by immigrants from Hong Kong who came to Canada to avoid the Chinese takeover of the former British colony in 1997. Taking advantage of their Vancouver connections, and cashing in their Asian fortunes, the new settlers purchased old homes, tore them down, and built the biggest homes that building codes would allow. Many of those who fled to Vancouver before 1997 have since returned to Hong Kong, although more recent immigrants from mainland China and elsewhere continue to maintain the monster-home "tradition."

witnessed any number of be-ins and demonstrations. When the entire city was virtually shut down by antiwar protests in March and April 1967, Kitsilano was the heart of the action. In the 21C, the neighbourhood still leans heavily leftward; some of those same activists are now long-term residents who have raised their families here.

Bordering Vanier Park along the English Bay shore, Kitsilano is paradise for those who love the outdoors. Neighbourhood amenities include Kitsilano Beach, Vancouver's largest outdoor pool, sand volleyball courts, a walking-biking-in-line skating path, and easy access to downtown—a 20-minute walk across the **Burrard Bridge**.

Craftsman-style Gems

You'll find some of Canada's best examples of Craftsman-style residential architecture in serene Kitsilano. The biggest and best ones are near **Vanier Park** (*between Chestnut and Arbutus Sts., north of Cornwall St.*).

SHAUGHNESSY

Bounded by Granville St., W.12th Ave., Oak St.and W. 33rd Ave.
This is Vancouver's original **mansion district**, a sublime hill where the city's first tycoons (such as timber baron H.R. MacMillan) who made their fortunes in the lumber, rail and trade industries, built stone and timber mansions in the early 20C. Curving streets (the city's first) wind past **palatial homes** of granite and fir, with broad lawns, semicircular drives, perfectly trimmed hedges and spreading oaks and maples. It looks like the baronial English neighbourhood it was intended to be when it was developed by the Canadian Pacific Railway in 1907. Although this isn't the priciest real estate in the Vancouver area any more (that title goes to the West Vancouver waterfront), a drive along Shaughnessy's quiet streets still produces its share of "oohs" and "ahhs." Descendants of the original residents now share their neighbourhood with Hollywood stars who rent homes here during film shoots.

LANDMARKS

You'll recognize Vancouver's cityscape by the blue-glass and brushed-metal style of the buildings that line the waterfronts along False Creek and Coal Harbour. Most of the city's landmarks date from the 20C, as Vancouver was founded in 1886, but a ferocious fire destroyed much of it shortly after it was incorporated. Whereas Gastown *(see Historic Sites)* preserves the city's pre-1900 buildings, the finest examples of contemporary architecture are downtown, along a one-mile loop that makes an easy walk. So put on your sneakers and sunglasses—the glare off the glass buildings on a sunny day can be fierce—and look at the landmarks that define this international city.

LANDMARK BUILDINGS

Canada Place★★

999 Canada Place Way, at the foot of Howe St. 604-665-9000. www.canadaplace.ca. Promenade open 24hrs daily. FlyOver Canada shows every 15min, 10am–9pm; $20.00.

You can't help but notice the white "ship" moored in **Burrard Inlet**. After almost a quarter-century, it has become an icon of Vancouver. The graceful canvas "sails" of Canada Place lift 70m/230ft above the water below.

Designed by Zeidler Partnership Architects, headed by Eberhard Zeidler, Canada Place opened in 1986. Built by the federal government for Expo '86, the structure acted as Canada's pavilion during the fair, and for the 2010 Olympics, it served double duty as the press centre.

Aside from their reference to the city's lifelong connection to maritime affairs, the **roof peaks,** held aloft by central pillars, make room for large open areas within the city's convention centre underneath.

With massive cruise ships docked alongside, the whole structure is eminently practical, no matter how fanciful it appears.

Head up to the second-level 🚶 **promenade** for wonderful **views★★** of the harbour, Stanley Park and the North Shore mountains. The new **FlyOver Canada** virtual flight experience (604-620-8455) provides stunning (and visceral) views of the city and its surroundings, while the top-notch **Pan Pacific Hotel** *(see Hotels)* occupies the southwest corner of the building, next to the Vancouver World Trade Centre. A **pedestrian path** departs from the southwest corner to Stanley Park, which is about a 20-minute walk away.

Fast Facts

♦ Canada Place rests on 6,000 pilings, some of which are from a pier that has occupied this spot since the 1920s.

♦ A Teflon coating keeps the exterior fabric clean.

Library Square★★

350 W. Georgia St. 604-331-3603. www.vpl.ca. Open Mon–Thu

Canada Place

10am–9pm, Fri–Sat 10am–6pm, Sun 11am–6pm.

Is it a grandiose imitation of ancient architecture—or a memorable addition to the Vancouver landscape? Hardly anyone is neutral about this colourful design by famed Canadian architect Moshe Safdie. Safdie denies the building's similarities to the **Roman Colosseum**—but the resemblance is obvious to almost everyone else. Made of brown pre-cast concrete, the complex opened in 1995, and houses the main Public Library, government offices, retail shops and a splendid **outdoor plaza** that's great for **people-watching** on sunny days. Nay-sayers who find the whole thing too much should glance across the street, at the Vancouver Post Office *(on the north side of Georgia St.)*.

Library Lowdown – The seven-level Public Library is one of the largest anywhere, with 1.2 million items, a large children's library, extensive audio-visual and electronic materials sections, and numerous nooks and crannies that are specifically designed to provide private reading spots. **Sky bridges** that span the seven-storey **atrium** are guaranteed to wrinkle the brows of anyone with acrophobia. The ground floor holds coffee shops, cafes and small retailers.

BC Place Stadium★
777 Pacific Blvd. 604-669-2300. www.bcplacestadium.com.
Though some have derided its appearance as a puff pastry left

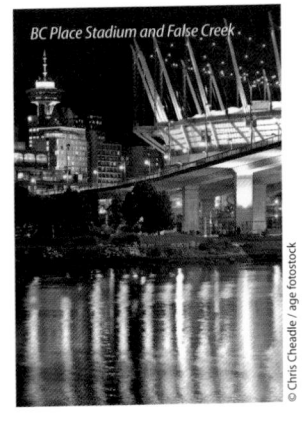

BC Place Stadium and False Creek

LANDMARKS

45

out too long – and admittedly, the bland utilitarian building is deeply unattractive – this fabric-dome-roofed structure has served its role admirably since 1983. More recently it was an essential element of the 2010 Winter Olympics for opening and closing ceremonies, and medal presentations. (Olympic bid organizers pointed out that using BC Place would alleviate fears of rain-drenched ceremonies at a snow-sports extravaganza.) Now sporting a new cable-supported **retractable roof**, said to be the largest roof of its kind on earth, the 55,000-seat stadium is home to the **BC Lions** Canadian Football League team, and a venue for rock and pop concerts, car and home shows and the like.

BC Sports Hall of Fame and Museum★
In BC Place. See For Kids.

Cathedral Place
[D] refers to map on the inside front cover. 925 W. Georgia St. at Hornby St.

This 1990 office tower was expressly designed to blend with its historic companions— the copper roof and gargoyles mimic the **Hotel Vancouver** across Georgia Street, and the Art Deco touches reflect the 1920s building it replaced. Ground-floor stonework, meanwhile, corresponds to **Christ Church Cathedral** to the west.

Christ Church Cathedral★
690 Burrard St. at Georgia St. 604-682-3848. www.cathedral. vancouver.bc.ca. Open before and after worship services, for concerts, and Mon–Fri 10am–4pm.

Outside, solid sandstone. Inside, massive hewn timbers bracing the roof. Though this is the seat of the Anglican diocese of Vancouver (it became a cathedral in 1929), it was built in 1889 to remind its members of parish churches back in Britain. The edifice is now the **oldest church** in the city, from a time when the area was residential. Its steep, **gabled roof**, arched windows and huge stained-glass windows are architectural treasures.

The church is frequently the site of concerts and other performances, both religious and secular. Plans to demolish the cathedral and sell the land for an office tower aroused a huge controversy in the late 1970s. In the end, the Episcopal diocese sold the density rights to the land to the developers of Cathedral Place just north *(see sidebar)*, allowing that building to rise taller, and gaining money for renovation of the church.

Harbour Centre Tower★
555 W. Hastings St.

Even after a quarter-century, this ungainly 167.5m/550ft landmark on West Hastings Street is, at 45 storeys high, Vancouver's second-tallest building, after the 62-storey Living Shangri-La was erected in 2008. The circular pod atop the tower houses a **viewing platform** and restaurant *(see For Fun)*; you can access it via a glass-walled elevator. The late astronaut Neil Armstrong

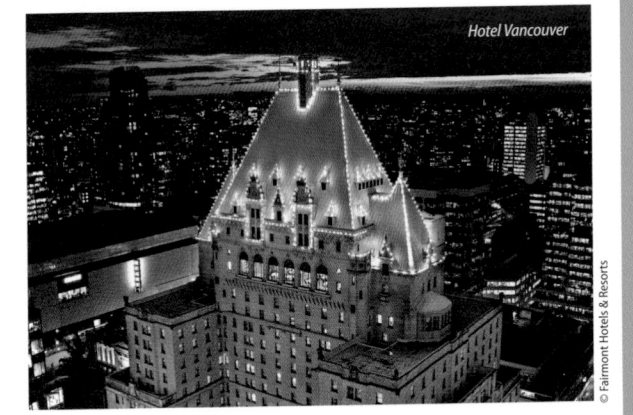

Hotel Vancouver

officially opened the building in August 1977, leaving behind—you guessed it—a footprint.

Hotel Vancouver★

900 W. Georgia St., between Burrard and Hornby Sts. 604-684-3131. www.fairmont.com/ hotelvancouver.

A city icon, the "Hotel Van" is one of the continent-wide chain of massive, château-style hotels built by Canadian railroad companies in the late 19C and early 20C. Its **copper roof** and gabled tower are often photographed to symbolize Vancouver.

Built by the **Canadian National Railway** and opened in 1939, the hotel was later taken over by Canadian Pacific, and it's now operated by the Fairmont chain, which invested millions of dollars in renovations in the 1990s. Special attention was devoted to the brushed-metal and glass Art Moderne touches in the lobby, which is worth a visit just to experience the atmosphere in one of the world's landmark hotels *(see Hotels)*

Law Courts and Robson Square★

800 Robson St., between Hornby and Howe Sts.

The Babylonian-style hanging gardens, suspended pools and waterfall freshets of this seven-storey complex make it hard to grasp the fact that it is indeed a single building. And despite its aesthetic appeal, serious business does take place inside this structure housing the provincial law courts ("law courts" is a term for **courthouse**).

Designed by Arthur Erickson, the facility you see here today was not the one originally intended for this site. A massive 55-storey tower was planned in the early 1970s, but never realized. The hundreds of workers, visitors and residents you'll see enjoying the Law Courts' **outside spaces** on a sunny day can attest to the wisdom of that decision.

There's also an **ice rink** for winter skating, and small garden patches at various levels with something in bloom virtually year-round.

Sun Tower
100 W. Pender St.
Newspaper publisher Louis Taylor aimed for extravagance with this towering edifice. At 17 storeys, it was tallest in the British Empire for a brief two years, from 1912 to 1914; the copper dome is an example of Beaux Arts design. And the nine half-clad buxom maidens (caryatids) that adorn the top storeys, where gargoyles are usually found, were meant to prick modest Edwardian sensibilities. They did.

Marine Building ★
355 Burrard St. at Hastings.
Money was no object for the builders of this elaborate structure, who intended it to be one of the snazziest buildings in North America. Sightseers who still gawk at it agree they succeeded: the terra-cotta frieze over the entrance, the phantasmagoric "Mayan" tilework in the lobby, the massive, figured-brass elevator doors—all are palatial in colour and form and sing of a bygone day when style was as important as function (or budget).

When it opened in 1930, the 21-storey building was the tallest in the British Commonwealth; today it's overshadowed by modern office towers, but none can match its flair. Exterior ornamentation illustrates Vancouver's maritime history, with clipper ships and marine creatures such as sea horses crowding the **entranceway frieze**. The blue, green and maroon tile and brass **lobby** is a fanciful representation of the inside of a Mexican temple. It could be said that the whole building was a fanciful business enterprise—the structure was finished at $2.3 million, almost 100 percent over budget. Its builders quickly went broke, and the Marine Building was sold to the Guinness family for $900,000 in 1933. A mosaic in the lobby floor depicts the Zodiac—you might say the building was born under a bad sign—in the midst of the Great Depression. Today it's a historic jewel.

Orpheum Theatre ★
884 Granville St.
See Performing Arts.

Former Eaton Building
701 Granville St. at Robson St.
604-685-7112.
This massive 1970s building is monumental in several ways. Its bulbous, light-shaded tubular shape has earned it a nickname drawn from classic literature: the "Great White Whale." It was the downtown **Eaton store** until that longtime Canadian chain went bankrupt in 1999. Sears took it over, and reconfigured the Eaton retail persona, which quickly flopped. Sears has moved out, and **Pacific Centre** plans to redevelop the space (*see Pacific Centre p50*). An industrious Irishman, one **Timothy Eaton**, immigrated to Canada when he was 22 years old. In 1869 he opened his first department store, locating it in Toronto and offering a new incentive to customers—the **money-back guarantee**. Before long, he established a second store in Toronto as well as a mail-order business, and the chain spread

With a constant stream of film and TV productions in the Vancouver area, many city landmarks have served as sets for films—often standing in for other structures of various sorts. The **Vancouver Art Gallery**, for instance, was used as the courtroom for the key scenes in *The Accused*, in which Jodie Foster won her first Academy Award. **Gastown** was transformed into Helena, Montana, for *Legends of the Fall*, with Brad Pitt and Anthony Hopkins. The **Hotel Vancouver's** green copper roofs became European in the film *Russian Roulette*. And, of course, a West End apartment house was Agent Sculley's Washington, DC, home during the eight-year run of the popular TV show *The X-Files*. The Vancouver area landscape also serves to represent locales around the world when Hollywood comes calling. Most famously, the deep woods around **Hope**, at the east end of the Lower Mainland, were the setting for *First Blood*, the kick-off film in the Rambo series that helped make Sylvester Stallone an international star.

from there. The holiday season brought wonderful **mechanized displays** in Eaton department store windows. In 1905, Eaton's introduced its Santa Claus Parade, which became the largest parade in North America by the 1950s, televised to a world audience of some 30 million viewers.

Holy Rosary Cathedral
646 Richards St. at Dunsmuir St. 604-682-6774. www.holyrosary cathedral.org. Open Mon–Sat

The Pendulum
HSBC Building, Georgia and Hornby Sts. www.885west georgia.com.
Shades of Edgar Allen Poe. One of the best-known pieces of public art in Vancouver, this 15m/50ft-long brushed-steel sculpture swings above the three-storey atrium lobby of the building's namesake bank. Vancouver artist Alan Storey created the piece in 1985.

8:30am–4:30pm; services on Sundays.
Once the tallest fir on the early Vancouver skyline occupied this spot. Now a 66m/217ft **steeple** holds its place, and the 15 large **stained-glass windows** dapple light inside much as old-growth forests do. One of the windows *(to the left of the altar)* was actually made in Paris in 1896, before the church was built.
The Gothic Revival-style building was finished in 1900, and declared a cathedral 16 years later. Pope John-Paul II sang Mass here in 1984; a contrast is presented by the small army of street people who spread their sleeping bags beneath the open atrium on the cathedral's south side.

Sinclair Centre
757 W. Hastings St., at Granville St. www.sinclaircentre.com.
Four historic buildings were melded into a modern shopping complex in this exemplary adaptation. The old Post Office (1910), Customs Warehouse, Federal Building and

Winch Building—all imposing Edwardian stone structures—have been joined by an interior **atrium-courtyard** that houses shops and cafes. Among the 20 retail stores is the classy, upscale fashion boutique **Leone**.

Pacific Centre
700 W. Georgia St., at Granville St. www.pacificcentre.ca.
Two blocks south, Pacific Centre is the modern version of the Sinclair Centre. It is an entirely underground **shopping mall** with 100 shops that stretches three city blocks north and south between Granville and Howe streets. Theoretically, guests at the Four Seasons Hotel need never go outside to shop. The mall's anchor store is **Holt Renfrew**, an **upscale apparel** chain *(604-681-3121; www.holtrenfrew.com)*, and a huge food court supplies nourishment to hungry shoppers. Pacific Centre is in the process of redeveloping the adjacent former Eaton Building *(Granville St. at Robson)* into a mixed-use complex that will include office space and a **Nordstrom** department store.

Olympic Cauldron
1055 Canada Place, Vancouver waterfront, next to the Convention Centre.
This spectacular 10-metre-high **Olympic torch** was lit by Canadian hockey legend, Wayne Gretzky, at the opening ceremony of the 2010 Winter Olympics; it stands as a monument to the Games, and a point of artistic fascination on the waterfront. Situated in Jack Poole Plaza, the space and Cauldron are dedicated to Jack Poole, chairman of the board for the Vancouver

Olympic Committee. Sadly, Poole died in 2009 and never witnessed the fruits of his efforts.

Olympic Village Seawall
False Creek, Creekside Park.
Built to aid pedestrian movement during the 2010 "Sea to Sky" Winter Games in 2010, the seawall could just as appropriately have been called the "sea walk." Linking neighbourhoods from Granville Island to the Yaletown seawall connection, the 3.84km (2.38mi) path is a scenic paradise for cyclists, joggers and walkers, passing by Science World British Columbia, the Olympic athlete residences (now condominiums), and along False Creek.

LANDMARK BRIDGES

Burrard Street Bridge
Burrard St., crossing False Creek.
This five-lane 1932 Art Deco-style span over **False Creek** comprises an arched gateway to downtown Vancouver. The decorative frieze on the stucco arch reads "By Land and Sea We Prosper." Stroll across the bridge at sunset to enjoy the expansive **views** of the western horizon and sundown light on the glass towers along False Creek. Residents use the bridge, and the south end of Burrard Street, as a shortcut to the airport and the highway to Seattle, bypassing the retail congestion of South Granville Street.

Lions Gate Bridge
North end of Stanley Park Causeway, linking Vancouver to the North Shore, crossing the Burrard Inlet.

© Brent Hannon / Michelin

Burrard Street Bridge

It's hard to believe, today, that this soaring structure was built with private funds. The **Guinness family** used proceeds from their brewing enterprises to provide access to North Shore property developments, opening the bridge in 1938.

The BC government bought it for $6 million in 1963, and at the end of the 20C, the span's increasing inability to handle all the traffic spurred numerous proposals to replace or expand it—ranging from adding another deck to building a tunnel beneath the entire downtown Vancouver peninsula. In the end, superficial improvements were made, and all other plans abandoned.

Today traffic crosses on three reversible lanes. The suspension bridge's main span stretches 472m/1,440ft, and the deck sits 61m/180ft above the water. It's also called the **First Narrows** bridge, after the passage it crosses. In 2005, the Government of Canada declared the Lions Gate Bridge a National Historic Site.

Second Narrows Bridge
On Hwy. 1, across Burrard Inlet at the second narrows.

This six-lane lift bridge (the highway is balanced out over the water, rather than suspended from cables) was built in 1960. It spans some 323m/1,060ft. During construction a part of the north arm span collapsed, killing 18 workers; in 1994 the bridge was renamed the **Ironworkers Memorial Bridge**.

Its original name (still in common use) refers to the fact that it crosses the second neck in Burrard Inlet; the Lions Gate Bridge spans the first. The 1925 dedicated railway lift bridge runs parallel to it.

Capilano Suspension Bridge
See Nearby Vancouver.

LANDMARKS

MUSEUMS

The unique history and culture of Pacific Canada are what distinguish Vancouver's best museums—Native totem poles and crafts, seafaring history, singular artworks that depict the stunning BC landscape. The number of noteworthy museums in Vancouver may be modest, but you'll find collections here that can't be found anywhere else on earth.

🏛 UBC MUSEUM OF ANTHROPOLOGY★★★

6393 N.W. Marine Dr., on the University of British Columbia campus. 604-822-5087. www.moa. ubc.ca. Open mid-May–early Oct daily 10am–5pm (Tue until 9pm); rest of year Tue–Sun 10am–5pm (Tue until 9pm). Closed Dec 24 & 25. $16.75; Tue eve $9.

Known the world over for its vast collection of aboriginal works— and the sensational building that houses them—the Museum of Anthropology (MOA) is one of North America's most important cultural institutions. It's also a great place to spend an afternoon looking at wonderful things. Designed by renowned Canadian architect Arthur Erickson, the

cast-concrete building rests atop a bluff overlooking the Strait of Georgia. From the outside, its huge concrete frame mimics a First Nations longhouse. As you descend a ramp into the main gallery, the roof rises, providing ever-taller halls for the totem poles that form the centrepiece of the museum's 38,000-item collection.

Great Hall

The museum's main gallery boasts ground-to-ceiling curtain-glass walls that let in every bit of available daylight. Massive 🏛 **totem poles** draw your attention first—almost all the Northwest Coast First Nations are represented, but the most prominent are the Haida,

UBC Museum of Anthropology

MUST SEE

Raven and the First Men (1980) by Bill Reid

© Leslie Forsberg / Michelin

Kwakwaka'wakw, Nisga'a and Coast Salish, in whose hands the art of carving totem poles reached its peak in the late 19C. Ravens, whales, eagles, salmon, bears, wolves and countless other creatures carved into the cedar logs demonstrate the Native peoples' affinity for the natural world that sustained them. **Smaller pieces**—bentwood cedar boxes, plaited-reed baskets, ceremonial masks—show the skill of figured designs that make Northwest Coast art distinctive.

Visible Storage Galleries

You'll find one of the world's most important collections of aboriginal artifacts here. Almost 14,000 objects are displayed in cases for visitors to see, in what the museum calls "visible storage."

Koerner Ceramics

This glistening 600-plus piece collection of European ceramics poses an intriguing contrast to the massive wood works just outside—both are beautiful and skillfully made, but utterly different in style.

Bill Reid Rotunda

The museum is also the most important repository for the work of famed **Haida artist** Bill Reid *(see sidebar, below)*. Reid helped create some of the poles and longhouses outside the museum in its representation of a traditional **coast village**. Stroll these paths, past alder groves, with totem poles peering down, and sense the silent spirits that inhabit BC's coast. Inside, small and large pieces include a fine selection of Reid's **jewellery,** and a **canoe** carved in the traditional fashion, with placards showing how it was done. Lustrous and haunting, **Raven and the First Men** is the work universally considered Reid's masterpiece. A depiction of the Haida creation myth, this sculpture has its own separate gallery at the museum. Reid carved it from a four-ton cedar block, and it was dedicated by Prince Charles in 1980. The work rests in a bed of sand brought by the Haida people from the beach in the Haida Gwaii Islands, where, according to Haida legend, on this very sand the Raven opened the clamshell in which humanity huddled, freeing the first men to discover the world. A recent addition (2012) to the Bill Reid Rotunda is a donation of 11 intricate pieces of **gold and silver jewellery** that the artist crafted from 1954 to 1974, which illustrate his experimentation with European goldsmithing techniques.

Bill Reid

A Canadian national treasure, Bill Reid (1920–1998) is one of those artists whose work is firmly rooted in his cultural heritage, but transcends it completely. The Haida are the ancestral people of Haida Gwaii (formerly the Queen Charlotte Islands), whose mist-clad, high-timbered shores evoke both the forces of nature and the spirits of vanished lifestyles. Reid was born in Victoria (his mother was Haida) and paid little attention to his heritage until he visited his grandfather in the islands in 1943. That visit fired his interest in traditional Haida carving, and he abandoned a career in radio. Reid's 40-year life as an artist encompassed works both big—totem poles and canoes—and small, such as finely-wrought gold and silver jewellery. His pieces reside in collections around the world, but his fame rests on the large works he did on commission late in life. A massive sculpture of a canoe bearing the earth's creatures decorates the International Terminal at Vancouver International Airport; a breaching killer whale greets visitors to Vancouver Aquarium; and a huge wooden bear sits in the Museum of Anthropology's Great Hall.

Haida Bear (1963) by Bill Reid, UBC Museum of Anthropology

© Museum of Vancouver

🦀 MUSEUM OF VANCOUVER★★

1100 Chestnut St., in Vanier Park. 604-736-4431. www.museumof vancouver.ca. Open mid-May–early Oct daily 10am–5pm (Thu until 8pm); rest of year Tue-Sun 10am–5pm (Thu until 8pm). Closed Dec 25. $14.

A huge **stainless-steel crab** stands at the entrance to the city's oldest museum. Sculptor George Norris fashioned it to symbolize the creature that guards the harbour in First Nations lore. Inside, the city's Native traditions and modern history come to life through a collection of some 70,000 items, ranging from First Nations ceremonial masks and 5,500 toy soldiers to neon signs from Vancouver's heyday as a capital of this commercial art. Founded in 1894, the Museum of Vancouver now shares a complex with the **H.R. MacMillan Space Centre★** (*see For Kids*); the building's cone-shaped roof mimics a Salish cedar rain-hat. Permanent collections are displayed in

decades, making it easy to explore the last century of Vancouver life.

Neon Vancouver/ Ugly Vancouver

The neon sign collection is a colourful, evocative throwback to the days of Vancouver's flashy big-city lights of the 1950s, 60s and 70s. The diverse assemblage evokes the former controversy over Vancouver's self-image. During the three decades in question, Vancouver hosted as many as 19,000 neon signs, a truly blinding array. Supporters of the glitz believed the signs embodied **big-city glamour**; detractors said they cheapened Vancouver and eclipsed its natural beauty. Witness for yourself Vancouver's public persona as portrayed in neon **retail signs** like Chez Paris, the Drake Hotel and Owl Drugstore, in every colour, size and typeface.

1900s-1920s: The Gateway to the Pacific

Like today, Vancouver of the early 20C saw lifestyle hype, inflated real

MUSEUMS

Neon Vancouver, Museum of Vancouver

estate and vast cultural diversity. During this three-decade window, Vancouver evolved from its modest roots to **big-city status**. The street-car network was expanding, allowing new residential enclaves access to the city's core. Despite the prejudices that typified the era, the world came to Vancouver's doorstep, seeking new beginnings.

Family Fun at the Museum of Vancouver

The Museum of Vancouver offers **special programs** for family enjoyment. Here are suggested activities for some of the permanent exhibits that make for a fun day for families at the museum:

1930s-1940s: Kids and their parents can be children all over again as they play with toys from yesteryear, comparing toys of that era to modern ones, and even having a go at making olden-day toys.

1950s - The 50s Gallery: Like the rest of the post-war world, Vancouver had toned down certain expectations and adjusted its goals to the sensibility of the "new frontier" and a return to core values. Find out how Vancouver's avenues, formerly dominated by street cars, were remade to accommodate the new propensity toward personal vehicles, and watch those controversial neon lights take over the town. Learn how up-and-coming neighbourhoods were established, and what went on at night in Gastown.

1960s-1970s You Say You Want a Revolution: Try on a few psychedelic hippie costumes. Parents can explain to their kids why they (or their parents) engaged in local and large-scale rebellion. Largely thanks to its moderate climate, Vancouver drew hippies from across Canada—and the world—as their gathering place; they left an indelible mark that exists today. You'll be surprised to learn that upscale Kitsilano was once a hippie haven with a peace symbol on every door. Check out the history of enviro-friendly groups like Greenpeace and how they got their start here back in the groovy days.

Emily Carr

Born in Victoria, Emily Carr (1871–1945) found her greatest success in the more cosmopolitan Vancouver, where she lived for a while as a young woman, and formed her lifelong disdain for artistic and social convention. The city's art museum was one of the few institutions to show her work during her lifetime, so when Carr died she willed almost all her works to the Art Gallery, which hangs a rotating selection of about two dozen canvases. Carr's brooding, dark-hued portraits of her homeland's rain forests, and the vanishing aboriginal life within them, are so distinctive that her paintings are instantly recognizable. Much of her work depicts First Nations life and draws its style from that motif—*Big Raven*, for instance, resembles the raven's representations on totem poles. Carr is often classed with Frida Kahlo and Georgia O'Keeffe, artists with whom she shared personal and cultural perspectives.

Period costumes, documents, photographs, models and artifacts make concrete the city's "golden years" as well as its **economic challenges** and the coming of World War I in 1914.

1930s–1940s: Boom, Bust, and War

Black and white photographs, artifacts, documents and re-created settings enliven topics such as the **city's origin** and the financial **crash of 1929**. In that same year, Vancouver merged with the neighbouring towns of South Vancouver and Point Grey to create Canada's third-largest city. Discover a Vancouver in the throes of economic depression. Saved by Canada's involvement in World War II in 1939, and the resulting economic upswing, the country found its factories and shipyards productive again.

1950s: The 50s Gallery

Exhibits reflect the breezy lifestyle of Vancouverites in the post-war era. Check out the re-created **living room** setting complete with a TV

and other "modern" amenities. Displays of **period clothing** call to mind Betty Crocker attired in apron, skirt and high heels. Play tunes on the large **jukebox** and 45rpm vinyl records. Recall the days of soda fountains and Chubby Checker when you visit this space.

1960s–1970s: You Say You Want a Revolution

Tie-dyed clothing, fringed and beaded, brings visitors back to the two decades of the **love, peace and freedom movement**. T-shirts, posters, banners and buttons capture the essence of the protest era. Hear rock songs and see films about rock bands of the time.

VANCOUVER ART GALLERY★★

750 Hornby St., at Robson St. 604-662-4719. www.vanartgallery. bc.ca. Open daily 10am–5pm (Tue until 9pm). Closed Jan 1 & Dec 25. $20; Tue eve by donation.
This stately building is Pacific Canada's leading art institution: it represents the work of BC's two best-known architects, and it

has the largest collection of the province's most famous artist—**Emily Carr** *(see sidebar)*. Designed by **Francis Rattenbury**, designer of Victoria's Parliament Buildings in *(see Excursions)*, the structure served as the Vancouver Courthouse from 1911 to 1974. It was recast in 1983 as an art museum by **Arthur Erickson**, who transformed the **rotunda** into a core of light along the centre of the building. Hung here are works by modern BC artists such as Stan Douglas, Rodney Graham and Jeff Wall, as well as works by Carr and Group of Seven artists.

Grounds for Dissension

The museum **grounds** are as dynamic as the art inside. Various parts of the building and its plaza and fountains outside have served as the settings for innumerable films. The steps on the southwest corner, facing Robson, are ground zero for protests in Western Canada—virtually no topic is too trifling for someone to set up a soapbox here; major controversies draw hundreds of demonstrators.

VANCOUVER MARITIME MUSEUM★★

1905 Ogden Ave., in Vanier Park. 604-257-8300. www.vancouver maritimemuseum.com. Open Victoria Day–Labour Day Tue–Sat 10am–5pm (Thur until 8pm); Sun noon–5pm. Rest of Year Tue–Sat 10am–5pm.; Sun noon–5pm. $11; by donation Thu evenings.

Vancouver's museum devoted to its maritime history sits, appropriately, on the shoreline at the entrance to False Creek. It offers an intriguing survey of the boats that plied the Northwest Coast, the people who sailed them and the reasons they did so. The museum was built as a BC centennial project in 1958.

St. Roch

The tent-like roof of the building shields the mast of a Royal Canadian Mounted Police patrol ship that was first to traverse the

Vancouver Maritime Museum

MUST SEE

🪶 A First Nations Welcome to YVR

It is not a museum per se, but Vancouver International Airport – or YVR, as residents call it – is richly decorated with carvings and sculptures, and is likely to provide visitors with their first sightings of local art, including two remarkable pairs of First Nations "Welcome Figures." International arrivals pass directly beneath the stern visages of two imposing 5.2m/17ft totem poles, a man and a woman, carved in red cedar and providing a traditional Coast Salish greeting. And in the arrivals hall, a pair of warmer, friendlier male and female figures, rendered in yellow cedar in the Clayoquot tradition, stand with arms raised in a time-honoured welcome to special events, such as, apparently, a flight into YVR.

Northwest Passage through Canada's Arctic in both directions. Amazingly enough, despite its career bashing through icy waters, the St. Roch is a **wood-hulled boat**—and a small one, at just 32m/104ft, built in a Vancouver shipyard in 1928. The schooner is permanently dry-docked inside the museum. You can clamber into and through the ship, marveling at the tight quarters its 10-man crew occupied while battling the Arctic during the ship's unprecedented World War II voyages. The first of these trips, from Vancouver to Halifax, took two years (1940–1942), during which the ship was twice trapped in sea ice.

Exploration History

In the rest of the museum, you'll discover Vancouver's lifelong ties to maritime affairs, from the canoes carved out of cedar by Native peoples to the late-18C Northwest voyages of European explorers. **Ship models** and descriptive exhibits and installations (the forecastle of a sailing ship, Captain George Vancouver's *Discovery*) illustrate often-rugged life at sea.

Shipping Today

A tugboat **pilothouse** represents present-day seafaring; the tug's wheel sits ready for children to turn. Exhibits explain the modern operations of Canada's busiest port.

H.R. MACMILLAN SPACE CENTRE★

See For Kids.

LANGLEY CENTENNIAL MUSEUM

9135 King St., in Fort Langley, just southwest of Fort Langley National Historic Site. 604-532-3536. www. museum.tol.ca. Open Mon–Sat 10am–4:45pm, Sun 1pm–4:45pm. Entry by donation.

Opened in 1958, the museum is a repository of artifacts that document the cultural heritage of the town and its people. Be sure to see the re-created **general store** and the excellent collection of **First Nations arts** and artifacts.

ROEDDE HOUSE MUSEUM

See Historic Sites.

HISTORIC SITES

Historic site or venerable landmark? Considering Vancouver's colourful history, it's sometimes hard to categorize. We've included a few historic must-sees here, but check out Chinatown as well as the Landmarks chapter for more great places with a past.

GASTOWN★

Water St., between Carrall and Richards Sts.

Vancouver's original site is now a **historic district** that has enjoyed a full-scale renaissance: housed in a fine collection of 19C buildings is an appealing assortment of 20C boutiques, cafes, souvenir shops, art galleries, pubs, and restaurants. The city's first **timber mills** began cutting wood here from nearby forests in 1862, and many of the brick and stone buildings in Gastown incorporate superstructures of old-growth Douglas fir timbers.

Rundown and slated for "urban renewal" by the 1950s, the area was revived and renovated thanks to citizen activism in the 1970s. Now a designated historic district, Gastown offers an authentic, atmospheric alternative to the city's more modern – and more homogenous – dine-and-drink neighbourhoods.

"Gassy" Jack

Pioneer life stories (or legends) have a tendency to be colourful, and Gassy Jack's is no exception. Born in 1830 in England, **Jack Deighton** went to sea at 14. He eventually wound up in the new colony of British Columbia, where he opened a saloon in New Westminster, up the Fraser River from present-day Vancouver. When that failed, he loaded a canoe with a bottle of whisky, a few sticks of furniture and a yellow dog and paddled to Burrard Inlet, where he began selling whisky to loggers at the new mill. In 1867 thirsty loggers helped him build the Globe Saloon—in 24 hours as legend has it—and Deighton's bar

Hotel Europe, Gastown

© Atlantide SNC / age fotostock

Interior, Waterfront Station

thrived. His nickname? Supposedly it refers to his never-failing willingness to tell a tale. A **statue** of Deighton stands in Maple Tree Square at Carrall and Water Streets.

Notable Buildings in Gastown

Byrnes Block
Water St., between Carrall and Abbott Sts.
An 1886 brick edifice decked out with pediments and pilasters, this block-long structure has several distinctions—it was one of the

city's first brick buildings, and it occupies the site on which "Gassy" Jack Deighton built his second saloon.

Gaoler's Mews
Water and Carrall Sts., across Water St.
The 19C customs house and jail now houses several First Nations art galleries.

Hotel Europe
Carrall and Water Sts., east of Maple Tree Square.
This 1908 poured-concrete structure no longer operates as a hotel, but it is one of the first of its kind in North America. All modern construction is required to blend with the district's heritage buildings.

WATERFRONT STATION
601 W. Cordova St., 604-953-3333. www.translink.ca.
Completed in 1914 this handsome, red-brick building overlooking Burrard Inlet, near Gastown, was once the passenger terminal for **Canadian Pacific Railway**. Its facade is distinguished by

---

Steam Clock
One of the most-photographed icons in Vancouver, this clock may look historic—indeed its mechanism harks back to the early Victorian era when steam powered all machinery—yet the Gastown clock is a modern artifact. It was built in 1977, representing a capstone to the district's restoration. The **whistle**, which sounds every quarter-hour, is steam-driven, but the clock is electric.

HISTORIC SITES

61

a colonnade and entryway of columns with Ionic capitals. The expansive flat roof is ringed by a balustrade.

After extensive renovation beginning in 1977, the station was transformed into a modern intermodal transportation facility. Today it serves as a departure point for SeaBus, SkyTrain and other Translink modes of transportation. Be sure to step inside the main concourse to view the **panels** painted with historic scenes of rail travel through Canada long ago. From here, a popular destination, Lonsdale Quay's **public market**, can be reached by a SeaBus ride across the harbour.

ROEDDE HOUSE MUSEUM

1415 Barclay St., West End.
604-684-7040. www.roedde
house.org. Open for tours May–
Aug Tue–Sun 11am–4pm.
Rest of the year Tue–Fri, and Sun,
1pm–4pm. $5 for guided tour;
$8 for Sun afternoon tea
and tour.

Quiet **Barclay Heritage Square**— just one block in size—and the neighbourhood surrounding it hint at the genteel quality of life that existed in Vancouver's **West End** a century ago. The highlight of this area is the opulent, fully restored 1893 Queen Anne Revival-style mansion, Roedde House. Built for Vancouver bookbinder Gustav Roedde and his family, the house is thought to have been designed by Francis Rattenbury, the architect responsible for the Parliament Buildings and the Empress Hotel in Victoria (*see Excursions*). The home's most distinctive feature is its rooftop **cupola**. It was from here, at the end of the 19C, that residents could watch the sea lanes for incoming vessels. Now, alas, West End development has blocked the view.

The 11 rooms in the **interior** of the house depict the middle-class lifestyle of an immigrant family in the late 19C. In the adjacent park you'll find a **Victorian garden**; visit in spring to see the rhododendrons in full bloom.

Parlour, Roedde House Museum

Forbidden Vancouver walking tour

City Walking Tours

One of the most popular tours for visitors to Vancouver, and local history buffs, is **Forbidden Vancouver**, a stroll through memory lane to spots like Gastown and Chinatown of the early 20C. Walkers follow "undercover newspaper reporter" Will Woods as he takes them through the **back alleys** of the city, and reveals its seedy side from long ago. Using wit and his penchant for history, England-born Woods, dressed in period costume as a journalist, informs and inspires by engaging walkers in the sordid stories that got him banned as a journalist way back when. Get there early; tours are limited to about 20 people.

Tue–Sat 6:30pm and 8pm in summer; Wed and Sat at 6:30pm, and Fri and Sat at 8pm in fall and spring; no tours in winter. $22. www.forbiddenvancouver.ca.

Wondering where the waterfront used to be in Yaletown, or why Francis Rattenbury had to hastily leave BC for England despite his fame as an architect? To learn the answer to these, and to learn more about the city's finest buildings, take a guided summer walking tour *(Jul and Aug, 10am and 1pm; about 2hrs; $10)* of one of six Vancouver (or Victoria) neighbourhoods offered by the **Architectural Institute of British Columbia** *(604-683-8588; www. aibc.ca/celebrating-architecture/ architectural-walking-tours/)*. Check the website for departure times and locations.

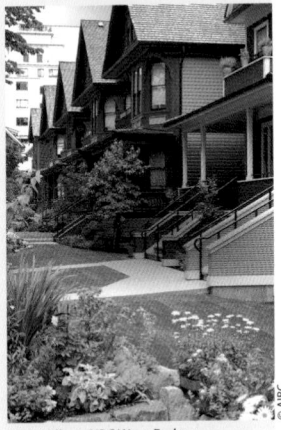

Mole Hill on AIBC West End tour

PARKS AND GARDENS

Green space is everywhere in Vancouver and its surrounding suburbs, from pocket-sized play areas to spacious natural areas of wetland and woods. The big city parks get the most attention, though, as forest-sized recreational areas like Stanley Park and the provincial parks on the North Shore offer beautiful views and places to play galore, along with a vast array of attractions ranging from gourmet restaurants to botanical gardens to broad sandy beaches.

STANLEY PARK★★★

At the northwest end of downtown, access via Georgia and Davie Sts. www.vancouver.ca/parks-recreation-culture/stanley-park.aspx. Open 24hrs daily.

Stanley Park is the unquestioned highlight of Vancouver, and one of North America's finest city parks. Urban residents are not only proud of their famous park, but they use it avidly—and visitors are just as fond of its attractions. It's big (405ha/1,000 acres), beautiful, accessible and uncrowded. A visit to Stanley Park can be as simple as a 20-minute stroll along the **seawall** path, or as elaborate as an interactive sea-mammal experience at the **Vancouver Aquarium★★★** (*see For Kids*) followed by a walk through **deep forests** to an elegant dinner at a restaurant overlooking the Strait of Georgia. Stanley Park has wildlife, woods, beaches, children's play areas, statues and 🖼 **totem poles**, and gardens and pools. Film crews use the park as a stand-in for woods worldwide.

You can accomplish a quick **driving tour** (*see Scenic Drive*) of the park in a morning, following the counterclockwise drive that skirts its perimeter and touches on most of the high points. However, it's best to set off **on foot**, or **by bicycle**, since much of the park's finest territory lies beyond the roadway. It's commonly assumed that Stanley Park's acres of Western red cedar, Douglas fir and Western hemlock are old-growth forest, but they're not: most of the park was logged before 1870 ("high-graded"—only the biggest and best timber was removed). The nearest true old-growth forest is across Burrard Inlet at **Lighthouse Park★★**. However, logging ceased so long ago in Stanley Park that much of its forest is now

---

A Park for the People?

In the late 19C Vancouver's first city council asked the federal government to preserve the land for Stanley Park and deed it to the city; it had been a military reserve, but it was not untouched forest. The transfer took place in 1888, and the park was dedicated the following year by its namesake, **Lord Peter Stanley**, Canada's governor-general. Though the city's founders showed amazing foresight to preserve such a magnificent piece of land, their motives were not wholly altruistic: the park was meant to boost the viability of housing developments in the West End.

Aerial view of Lions Gate Bridge and Stanley Park

approaching maturity. As you hike and bike along some of the interior trails, you'll see some impressively large trees—despite the loss of hundreds of trees in a violent wind storm in December 2006.

Visiting Stanley Park

It's advisable to arrive by bus or on foot, as **parking** can pose a problem; even if you can find a space, it costs up to $3 per hour (the pay meters must be fed; parking police are vigilant). Popular venues like Vancouver Aquarium, Totem Park, Prospect Point, Third Beach and Second Beach are the most crowded. If you can, arrive early, find parking, and walk to the sights. A stroll from Third Beach to the Aquarium, for example, takes just 15 to 20 minutes.

Other Tips

♦ Stop first at the **visitor centre,** which is located about .8km/.5mi in on Stanley Park Drive near the aquarium entrance, and pick up a map.

♦ Do not feed the cute squirrels, raccoons and other critters—they are wild and they can bite.

♦ If you want to swim, **Second Beach★** is best in the morning, and Third Beach is best in the afternoon.

♦ Use the free **park shuttle bus**: its makes 15 stops at popular destinations (*10am–6:30pm*).

Nature House

South side of Lost Lagoon, at northwest end of Robson St. 604-257-8544. www.stanleyparkecology.ca. Open Jul–Aug Tue–Sun 10am–5pm. Sept–Jun weekends 10am–4pm.

This compact facility is an interpretive centre for Stanley Park, operated by a local ecology organization. Periodic programs cover everything from the creatures that live in the lagoon to the life cycle of the old-growth forest that Stanley Park is becoming again. Volunteers are on-site to answer questions about the park and distribute information.

PARKS AND GARDENS

Scenic Drive★

The 10km/6mi drive that circles the park perimeter will take you past all of its significant sights. Traffic moves **counterclockwise**, starting at the park entrance at the end of West Georgia Street. Stanley Park Drive first swings around Coal Harbour, passing the Vancouver Rowing Club and Royal Vancouver Yacht Club. Between the two, to the north, is the entrance to the Vancouver Aquarium, and the main park **information kiosk**. A quarter-mile farther rises the park's famed collection of 🪶 **totem poles★** (see sidebar), occupying a site where a Coast Salish village stood 150 years ago.

Nine O'clock Gun

At **Hallelujah Point**, just past the totem poles, this gun is fired every evening—since 1894—to mark a historic fishing curfew. **Brockton Point** holds a replica of the prow of the *Empress of Japan*, one of the first clipper ships to call at the port

of Vancouver. Just past that, the Girl in a Wet Suit **statue**, placed on a rock in 1984, mimics the legendary mermaid sculpture that graces Copenhagen's harbour.

Prospect Point★

The road climbs to a bluff at Prospect Point, offering wide **views★** of the North Shore with snowcapped mountains behind, and across the Strait of Georgia to Vancouver Island. A half-mile farther on, stop at the **Hollow Tree**, a much-photographed cedar stump, to see how many people you can fit inside.

Third Beach★

This broad expanse of golden sand is perfect for picnicking and admiring the views. **Ferguson Point** offers more views from a bluff; and the Stanley Park Pool at **Second Beach★** is packed with sunbathers on warm days (see *Outdoor Fun*). The road winds by the park's excellent **pitch-and-**

🪶 Totem Poles★

Carved from cedar logs, totem poles are traditional Native monuments that depict the animals and spirits central to the First Nations' pantheistic belief systems. Ravens, bears, salmon, eagles, frogs, whales and wolves are common figures. An **interpretive centre** near the totem poles explains traditional Native village life, and a shop offers guidebooks and posters. Artists represented include Bill Reid (see *Museums*) and Chief Mungo Martin, two legendary Native carvers.

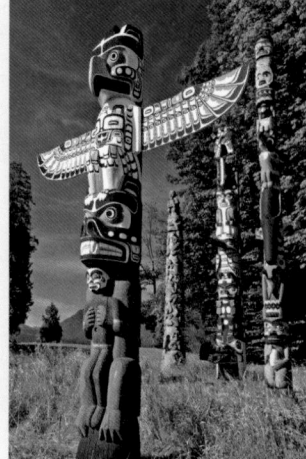

© Ulana Switucha / age fotostock

66

Photo Ops for Tree-Lovers

The **Hollow Tree**, along Stanley Park Drive a half-mile south of Prospect Point, was once sufficiently large enough that today its shell-like stump is one of the park's most famous photo ops, with groups of people posing inside the enormous trunk. Springboard notches on the side mark the place where loggers stood in the 1870s to bring down this huge cedar.

Other tree-related photo opportunities include, near the Third Beach concession, a **red alder** with four trunks that is reckoned to be the largest alder in Canada; and a **big-leaf maple** in the woods southeast of the Hollow Tree that is considered the largest such maple in the country.

Another cherished photo site, alas, is no more: in the 1950s the National Geographic Society declared a **Western red cedar** on the park's western slope the world's largest, thanks to a trunk that measured 3.6m/12ft in diameter. The tree fell during a windstorm in 2006, but Stanley Park still boasts a lot of big-treedom in a small area—imagine the trees that stood here before the park was logged!

putt golf course, bypassing **Lost Lagoon** (a slightly brackish pond) to return to Georgia Street.

Stanley Park Seawall★★

Ready for a walk? This marvelous 9.5km/6mi **bike and pedestrian path** was the lifework of stonemason James Cunningham (1878–1963). A 9.5km/5.9mi barrier of 46kg/101-pound granite blocks built over the course of 46 years to withstand the battering of winter storms, the seawall follows much the same route as the driving tour described here, but affords better views. At Prospect Point, watch for **Siwash Rock★**, a small sea stack that, according to Native legend, represents the petrified soul of a virtuous member of the Salish tribe.

Gardens

Flower aficionados will want to visit the lovely formal **rose gardens** (along Pipeline Rd.), which reach their peak in June,

and the **rhododendron gardens** (south of Lost Lagoon), where hundreds of different varieties burst into bloom in May and June.

Trails

A dozen well-maintained trails crisscross the interior of the park, offering hikers and bikers the opportunity to find solitude in the woods. **Lake Trail** and **Tatlow Walk** are two of the best; you can access them from Stanley Park Drive near Second Beach.

Carriage Tours

Horse-drawn trolleys depart Coal Harbour parking lot every half hour, Mar 15–Oct 31. *1hr tour $30. 604-681-5115. www.stanleyparktours.com.*

Vancouver Aquarium★★★, Children's Farmyard and Miniature Train

See For Kids.

VANDUSEN BOTANICAL GARDEN★★

5251 Oak St. at 37th Ave. 604-257-8335. vandusengarden. org. Open daily: Dec and Jan 10am–3pm; Feb and Nov 10am–4pm; March and Oct 10am–5pm; Sep 10am–6pm; Apr 10am–7pm; May 9am–8pm; Jun–Aug 9am–9pm. Dec Festival of Lights 4:30pm–9pm. Oct–Mar $7.75, Apr–Sept $10.75. Closed Dec 25.

Imagine houses filling this lovely spot, instead of the colourful botanical garden–that's the fate this land nearly suffered. Once the site of a golf club for the nearby Shaughnessy mansion district (*see Neighbourhoods*), the land that now holds VanDusen garden was slated to be turned into a residential housing development in the 1970s. **Citizen activism** spurred the city to buy the 55-acre piece of rolling ground, and it has since grown into a horticultural showpiece.

The garden's overall purpose is to demonstrate the horticultural possibilities offered by Vancouver's **mild climate**—a notion illustrated by the healthy copse of palms growing beneath mature Douglas firs and cedars by the entrance.

The wide variety (7,500 different plants) ensures that something is in bloom almost year-round. The gift shop and bookstore focus on material promoting horticulture in the Lower Mainland. Inside the garden, plantings range from hollies to bamboos, and magnolias to birches. Numerous **theme gardens** scattered about the site include a Japanese meditation garden, an herb garden, a perennial garden, a maze and a fern dell. Among the highlights are the following:

Winter Garden

This collection of fragrant witch hazels, winter hazels and winter-blooming jasmine, as well as hellebores and other exotic off-season bloomers, is enchanting in January and February, belying winter's gray skies.

Canadian Heritage Garden

Native Canadian plants here focus on those that clothed, housed and fed First Nations people and pioneers, ranging from red cedar to Saskatoon berries. Plants from both east and west, and the prairie in between, are included.

Autumn, Heron Lake, VanDusen Botanical Garden

QUEEN ELIZABETH PARK★

*33rd Ave. and Cambie St.
604-257-8400. vancouver.ca/
parks-recreation-culture/queen-
elizabeth-park.aspx.
Open 24hrs daily.*

The highest point in Vancouver, a 154m/505ft hillock, is the pinnacle of this 52.5ha/130-acre park, which spreads across the largely open hillside. Six million visitors a year make Queen Elizabeth the city's second most popular park. The northwest end of the park is an **arboretum** that holds almost all the trees native to Canada, as well as many specimens from Europe and elsewhere in North America. **Nat Bailey Stadium**, on the park's southern end, is the summer home of the Vancouver Canadians, the city's minor-league baseball team (*see Practical Information*).

Bloedel Floral Conservatory

At the park's high ground sits Bloedel Conservatory, a geodesic-style greenhouse that houses 500 tropical plants and fish, and 100 free-flying birds. Paths wander amid the gardens and aviaries. A plexiglass dome covers one of the largest domed greenhouses in the world.

Quarry Gardens

Occupying a former stone quarry, this multi-level garden with its colourful annuals and sweeping lawns brings to mind Victoria's Butchart Gardens, though it's not quite as formal (*see Excursions*).

Viewpoint

Climb to the city's highest point (154m/505ft) here for a wonderful

panorama★★ of Vancouver to the north, and the North Shore Mountains beyond—including the twin "Lions" peaks for which Lions Gate is named. To the east, you can see the vast snowy summit of Mount Baker, and in the west, the Georgia Strait and the mountains of Vancouver Island loom in the distance.

DR. SUN YAT-SEN CLASSICAL CHINESE GARDEN★

*578 Carrall St., Chinatown.
604-662-3207. vancouver
chinesegarden.com. Open May–
mid-Jun and Sept 10am–6pm; late
Jun–Aug 9:30am–7pm; Oct–Apr
10am–4:30pm; Dec 24 and 31
10am–3pm. Closed Mon Nov–Apr,
closed Dec 25 and Jan 1. $12.*

You're bound to find serenity amid the intricately laid patios, elaborately decorated pavilions and carefully positioned rocks of the Sun Yat-Sen garden. The stucco, tile-roofed walls of the compound shelter one of the finest formal gardens in North America.

Indeed, this was the first true Ming Dynasty-style garden built in North America.

In 1886 Chinese artisans crossed the Pacific to help create it, bringing with them classical stone, tile, brick and timber.

Like all Chinese gardens, this one focuses as much on the man-made framework for growing things, as on the plants themselves. Each plant is chosen for its symbolic meaning, and the garden celebrates all **four seasons** with azaleas and trees such as maples, magnolias and evergreens. **Moon gates** and open portals offer artful views into **courtyards** and meditation nooks. Frequent guided tours *(included in price of admission)* explain the painstaking construction and significance of every element, none of them random.

UBC BOTANICAL GARDEN★

6804 S.W. Marine Dr., on the University of British Columbia campus. 604-822-9666. www.botanicalgarden.ubc.ca. Open daily 9:30am–5pm. $9, or UBC Museums and Gardens Pass $33.

The largest **rhododendron** collection in Canada—400 varieties—nestles beneath the native hemlock trees in this 28ha/70-acre garden that melds Northwest species with horticultural plants. Theme gardens are scattered throughout the property. The setting, on a bluff overlooking the Strait of Georgia, adds to the pleasure of a visit. At the gift shop, you can buy seeds from some of the plants in the botanical garden,

The Palm Gardens

Vancouver's much-acclaimed "mild" climate is given exquisite testimony in several gardens near **English Bay Beach**, at the intersection of Denman and Davie streets. Here city horticulturists have planted several dozen palm trees and other tropical plants (including hardy bananas) that thrive in the protected, south-facing location. Though frosts do occur in the area, the waters of English Bay moderate the cold, and the West End high rises block the chilliest northerly winds. On a sunny summer day, with palm fronds waving in the breeze, you could almost believe you were in the Caribbean.

The Palm Gardens

and the shop also has gardening books, tools and accessories. The only drawback, rare in a botanical garden, is a lack of signs identifying the different plants.

Alpine Garden

Specimens from mountains around the world—from Borneo to Russia—are included in one of the largest alpine collections in North America.

Asian Garden

Magnolias (in fact, one of the largest collections on earth), rhododendrons and azaleas predominate in this sprawling garden in the shade of mature conifers.

Food Garden

Bearing everything from kiwis to kohlrabi, the raised beds and fruit borders of this garden illustrate what can be grown in household gardens.

Native Garden

You'll find hundreds of species native to the province in this plot.

Physic Garden

Both old and new medicinal plants are here, from yarrow and rose hips to periwinkle, source of a modern drug used to treat leukemia.

BC Rain Forest Garden

Filled with displays of native plants, this collection represents elements of the coastal rain forests of southwestern British Columbia and the Southern Interior Wet-belt.

Carolinian Forest

This new feature of the UBC Botanical Garden exemplifies Canadian and eastern North American deciduous hardwood forests.

Garry Oak

The Garry Oak Meadow and Woodland Garden is a new feature of the UBC Botanical Garden. It is a sustainable landscape, intended to thrive with minimal intervention, and featuring the signature tree of southern Vancouver Island.

UBC Greenheart Canopy Walkway

6804 S.W. Marine Dr., on the University of British Columbia campus, in the UBC Botanical Garden. 604-822-4208. www.botanicalgarden.ubc.ca/canopy-walkway. Open daily 10am–4pm. $20 includes admission to the UBC Botanical Garden.

Situated in the David C. Lam Asian Garden, the Greenheart Canopy Walkway is a 308m/1,010ft **aerial trail** system, the only one of its kind in Canada, that offers an intimate glimpse of the natural wonder of a typical west coast forest canopy ecosystem. This aerial concept sees guests traverse bridges suspended 50ft high, allowing access to the treetops, where they will delight at a thriving diversity of flora and fauna that inhabits the lofty environment. This is more than a stroll around the trees; it's an interaction with the forest and its inhabitants. *Hourly tours take about 45 minutes and are limited to 20 people per tour; they may be booked in advance.*

NITOBE MEMORIAL GARDEN

S.W. Marine Dr., on the University of British Columbia campus. Enter at Gate 4. 604-878-9274. www.botanicalgarden.ubc.ca/nitobe. Open Apr–Oct 9:30am–5pm. $7.

Inside the walls of this 1ha/2.5-acre enclave you'll find a carefully constructed Japanese garden that focuses on traditional elements of balance and serenity. Paths wander amid ponds, meditation gardens, azaleas, flowering cherries and irises. In the fall, the **Asian maples** bear brilliant crimson and orange leaves. Bridges, benches and carefully placed stones complete the meditative atmosphere. The garden honours Dr. **Inazo Nitobe** (1862–1933), a diplomat and longtime BC resident devoted to bridging the gap between Japanese and North American cultures. With its teahouse, the **Tea Garden** inside Nitobe is considered one of the most authentic outside Japan. "I am in Japan," proclaimed that country's former emperor when he toured the garden in the 1990s.

PACIFIC SPIRIT REGIONAL PARK

Between 4th Ave. and Marine Dr. in the Point Grey section of Vancouver, also south to Fraser River. Information centre at 4915 W. 16th Ave. 604-224-5739. www.metrovancouver.org. Open dawn–dusk.

This sprawling expanse of woods borders Southwest Marine Drive on its approach to the University of British Columbia campus. Its extensive network of 🥾 **hiking trails** (20km/33mi) and 🚲 **biking** trails (14km/23mi) includes many paths that lead downhill to the shore of English Bay, offering seclusion and sun-dappled forest. Along the way, Pacific Spirit meets **Jericho Beach Park** (a shoreline greenbelt that offers sandy beaches and picnic areas) and farther west toward UBC, **Wreck Beach**, a legendary expanse of sand where clothing is optional. On the more northerly stretches of bluff-bordered pebble shore, you'll have spectacular **views★★** of the North Shore Mountains.

With sections spreading south across the Point Grey Peninsula, the entire park at 763ha/1,885acres ranks as the **largest green space** in Vancouver—nearly twice as large as Stanley Park. Almost entirely logged in the 19C, it has since sprung up again into a lush forest in which a dozen kinds of ferns grow in the filtered light. The southeast end of the park includes **Camosun Bog**, a rare example of a once-common peat marshland.

NORTH SHORE PARKS

Here's a list of must-visit parks in North and West Vancouver. For detailed descriptions of individual sites, *see Nearby Vancouver.*

Lighthouse Park★★

Marine Dr., 8km/5mi northwest of downtown via Lions Gate Bridge; ◯ *Follow Marine Dr. west to Beacon Lane.*
This 79ha/185-acre park harbours one of the area's last major parcels of untouched **old-growth forest**. Its vantage point on a Howe Sound headland means you'll get stunning **views★★★** of Vancouver across the water.

Cypress Provincial Park★

12km/7mi northwest of downtown via Lions Gate Bridge & Hwy. 1 west to Cypress Mountain Rd.
Ski areas, fir and hemlock forests and breathtaking **views★★★** are highlights of the 3,000ha/7,400-acre recreational area.

Lynn Canyon Park★

17km/10.5mi north of Vancouver via Lions Gate Bridge to Hwy. 1. ◯ *Take the Lynn Valley Rd. exit, turn right on Lynn Valley Rd. and right on Peters Rd. to the park.*
This North Shore gorge boasts a 33m/109ft-long **suspension bridge★** and a spectacular waterfall and swimming hole.

Ambleside Park

6km/4mi north of Vancouver via Lions Gate Bridge and west on Marine Dr.
Locals favour this strip of green space interspersed with sandy beaches that starts at the Capilano River and hugs the shoreline for several miles west.

Capilano River Regional Park

9km/6mi north of Vancouver via Lions Gate Bridge to Hwy. 1 to Capilano Rd. ◯ *Take the exit for Grouse Mountain and continue north to the park.*
🏔 **Hiking trails** within this 142ha/350-acre regional park cross the river and climb into deep forest, offering occasional–but spectacular–mountain views.

NEARBY VANCOUVER

If you can tear yourself away from Vancouver proper, it's worth a sojourn to the Lower Mainland. This area stretches from the Strait of Georgia east to Hope and the Cascade Range, bounded on the south by the US border, and on the north by the southern flanks of the towering Coast Mountains.

Here you'll find everything from small, U-pick berry farms to spectacular canyons cutting through mountains. Home to some two million people, the **Lower Mainland** includes the Fraser River Delta, the lower Fraser Valley, and the foothills of both the Coast and Cascade ranges. Though it makes up just two percent of British Columbia's landmass, this region contains half the population of the entire province. Urban growth is a reality these days, but a lot of this land remains pastoral, relying on good soil and mild weather for its agricultural bounty.

NORTH AND WEST VANCOUVER

These two communities were developed as suburbs of Vancouver, but they now have small city centres, and their own parks, schools and governments. Residents are fond of pointing out that in one direction they have quick access to the city itself—and in the other, heading up into the **North Shore Mountains**, they have one of the biggest, wildest and most spectacular wilderness areas on the continent.

Lighthouse Park★★

Off Marine Dr., 8km/5mi northwest of downtown via Lions Gate Bridge; follow Marine Dr. west to Beacon Lane. 604-925-7275. www.westvancouver.ca/parks-recreation/parks/lighthouse-park. Open year-round daily dawn–dusk. This protected enclave on **Point Atkinson** at the westernmost end of West Vancouver has three wonderful facets: the Lower Mainland's largest remaining **old-growth forest**, inviting hiking

---

Tree-mendous

Douglas-fir isn't really a fir. Western red-cedar isn't a true cedar, either. And western hemlock doesn't have anything to do with what Socrates drank. Misidentification and accidents of history have created great confusion over the names of the most prominent forest trees of the Pacific Coast—but there's no confusion over their size, beauty and ecological significance. Douglas firs are usually the tallest trees, with thick, reddish-brown corrugated bark that withstands fire well. They can grow to 91.5m/300ft in height and 3m/10ft in diameter. Red cedars have fabric-like bark, drooping branches and foliage, and sturdy flared bases, and they favour wetter locations. Western hemlocks have smoother, thinner bark, and lacier foliage than Douglas firs, but approach similar size and age. A true, mature temperate rain forest, like the one in Lighthouse Park, has a mix of all three types, in various sizes and ages.

© Lijuan Guo / Dreamstime.com

Lighthouse Park

trails that lead through the woods down to the shore, and memorable **views★★★** of Vancouver from the rocky shoreline. The park's untouched woods have made it a popular location for film crews, for whom it has stood in for forests around the world.

Old-Growth Forest

Fortunately, the temperate rain forest that now forms part of the park was not logged during Vancouver's development. Today, the big trees (some up to 500 years old, with diameters approaching 2m/7ft) anchor a classic old-growth ecosystem. Huckleberries, vine maples, scrub oak and red-barked madrones (called arbutus in Canada) fill open spaces where soft light filters through the conifer canopy overhead.

⚓ Hiking in Lighthouse Park

Walking the park's paths, in the serene, light-dappled forest understory, hints at what the entire Lower Mainland was like before European settlement. The best path through the forest parallels the road on the west side of the peninsula *(follow signs to the outdoor theatre)*. Once you reach the **Point Atkinson Lighthouse** complex, shoreline trails lead east and west along the rocky beach.

Touring Tip

The **Lions Gate Bridge** *(see Landmarks)*, which joins North and West Vancouver to Vancouver proper via the Stanley Park Causeway, is just three lanes wide. It backs up considerably during the morning and evening commute. Though visitors are usually travelling the opposite direction, counter-commute traffic has only one lane on the bridge, so the trip may be no faster. Allow an extra 30 minutes if you are crossing during morning or evening rush hour.

NEARBY VANCOUVER

Howe Sound

© Nina Ignatova / Dreamstime.com

Sea to Sky Highway★★

Rte. 99 runs 102km/63mi from Horseshoe Bay in West Vancouver north to Whistler. www.britishcolumbia.com/plan-your-trip/regions-and-towns/vancouver-coast-mountains/sea-to-sky-highway. Sights below are organized from south to north.

Even if you don't want to follow Route 99 all the way to Whistler, be sure to drive along at least a part of this highway for incredible **views★★★** of the blue-green waters of the Howe Sound with mountains all around it. Extending some 48km/30mi into the Coast Mountains, between the picturesque ferry port of **Horseshoe Bay** and the town of **Squamish** to the north, this deep fjord provides some of the province's most dramatic coastal scenery.

Britannia Mine Museum★★

38km/24mi north of Horseshoe Bay on Rte. 99, in Britannia Beach. 604-896-2233. Open daily 9am–5pm. $25. www.britanniamine museum.ca.

This former copper mine, now a National Historic Site, enjoyed its heyday beginning in World War I, when Britain and her allies relied on its output. By 1929 it was the

Britannia Mine Museum

© Britannia Mine Museum

MUST SEE

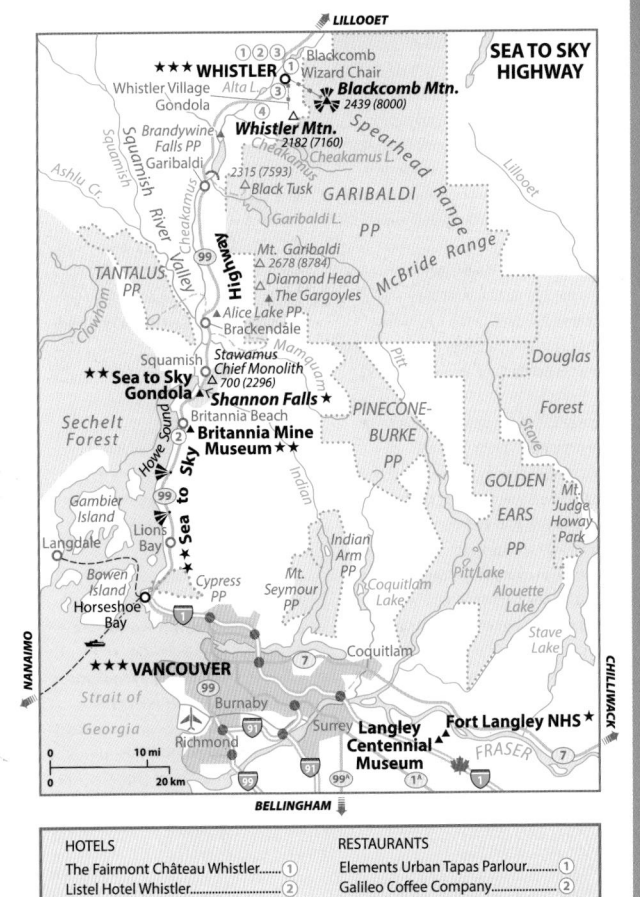

LILLOOET

★★★ **WHISTLER** ① ② ③
Blackcomb ① Wizard Chair
Whistler Village Alta L. ③
Gondola ④ ★★ *Blackcomb Mtn.*
2439 (8000)
Brandywine △ ★ *Whistler Mtn.*
Falls PP Cheakamus 2182 (7160)
Garibaldi 2315 (7593)
Spearhead Range
Ashlu Cr.
△Black Tusk **GARIBALDI**
(Garibaldi L. **PP**
McBride Range
Mt. Garibaldi
△ 2678 (8784)
TANTALUS ▲Diamond Head
PP ▲The Gargoyles
▲Alice Lake PP
Brackendale
Squamish ○ *Stawamus*
Chief Monolith **Douglas**
★★ **Sea to Sky** △ 700 (2296)
Gondola ▲ *Shannon Falls* ★ **PINECONE-**
Britannia Beach **BURKE**
Sechelt ▲ **Britannia Mine** **PP**
Forest **Museum** ★★
GOLDEN
Gambier **EARS** Mt.
Island Lions ○ **PP** Judge
Langdale Bay △ *Indian* Howay
Bowen ○ *Arm* Park
Island Cypress pp *PP* Pitt Lake
○ Mt.
Horseshoe Seymour Alouette
Bay PP *Coquitlam* Lake
○ *Lake* Stave
★★★ **VANCOUVER** Coquitlam Lake
Burnaby
Strait of ⑦
Georgia Surrey **Langley** **Fort Langley NHS** ★
Richmond **Centennial**
Museum **FRASER**

0 ___ 10 mi
0 ___ 20 km

BELLINGHAM

HOTELS		RESTAURANTS	
The Fairmont Château Whistler	①	Elements Urban Tapas Parlour	①
Listel Hotel Whistler	②	Galileo Coffee Company	②
Summit Lodge	③	Rimrock Cafe	③
Whistler Hostel International	④		

largest copper mine in the former British Empire. Closed in 1974, the mine now welcomes visitors who pile into ore cars for a trip into the 671m/2,200ft **supply shaft**. The eerie eight-level **concentrator building** has often served as a film set. Guided tours *(45min)* are highly recommended. Stop for coffee and pastries afterwards, at the nearby **Galileo Coffee**

Company *(173 Highway 99, Britannia Beach; 604-896-0272.)*

Shannon Falls★
45km/28mi north of Horseshoe Bay.
A short hike from the site's parking lot along Route 99 leads to a viewing point at the base of these impressive falls, which cascade 335m/1,100ft over a cliff here.

Sea to Sky Gondola★★

46km/29mi north of Horseshoe Bay on Rte. 99. 604-892-2550. Open May–Oct Sun–Thu 10am–5pm, Fri and Sat 10am–10pm; Dec–Apr Thu–Sun 10am–5pm; open daily during Christmas holidays. Closed Nov. www.seatoskygondola.com. $34.95.

This sparkling new addition to the Sea to Sky Highway – it opened in May 2014 – is more than a mere gondola ride, though that is adventure enough, lifting visitors 885m/2,900ft above Howe Sound. The subsequent suite of entertainment includes an extensive network of hiking trails, a pair of breath-taking sightseeing platforms, and the vertigo-inducing Sky Pilot suspension bridge. The complex caters to all tastes: back-country aficionados will like the easy access it provides to the high mountains, while more comfort-loving souls can tuck into a craft beer and a pulled pork sandwich at the West Coast-style **Summit Lodge,** while enjoying fine views of Howe Sound and the impressive granite face of nearby Stawamus Chief mountain.

Treetops Adventure, Capilano Canyon

Whistler★★★

See Excursions.

Capilano Canyon★

From Lions Gate Bridge, take Marine Dr. east to Capilano Rd., Exit 14, in North Vancouver. The suspension bridge entrance is at 3735 Capilano Rd. 604-985-7474. www.capbridge.com. Open May–Sept daily 8:30am–8pm. Rest of the year daily 9am–dusk. Closed Dec 25. $35.95.

🚡 Capilano Suspension Bridge Park★★★

Some 800,000 yearly visitors enjoy the gorgeous views from the **Capilano Suspension Bridge**, which rises 70m/230ft above the river, tucked close to a steep mountainside. Built in 1889 and rebuilt in 1956, the bridge measures 137m/450ft, and sways as visitors walk across it.

On the opposite side, **Treetops Adventure** encompasses seven suspension bridges and **viewing platforms** secured, without nails or bolts, to trunks of Douglas firs; some platforms sit 30m/100ft above ground. The new **Cliffwalk** is a series of glass-and-steel walkways suspended from the sculpted granite cliffs, which afford fine views of canyon, cliffs, and the surrounding emerald-green rain forests.

Cypress Provincial Park★

12km/7mi northwest of downtown Vancouver via Lions Gate Bridge and Hwy. 1 to Cypress Mountain Rd. 604-926-5612. www.env.gov.bc.ca/bcparks/ explore/parkpgs/cypress/. Open year-round daily.

© Eric P. Lucas / Michelin

Zip line at Grouse Mountain

© Grouse Mountain

Clinging to the heights of the **Coast Range** above West Vancouver, this ski- and snow-sports area was the site of the snowboard and freestyle events during the 2010 Winter Olympics. In summer, **hiking trails** lead through the western red-cedar and yellow cedar forests for which the 3,012-hectare/7,440-acre park is named. The access road leads to Highview Lookout, which permits a breathtaking **view★★** of the Vancouver area.

Grouse Mountain★
From Lions Gate Bridge, take Capilano Rd. to 6400 Nancy Greene Way, North Vancouver. 604-980-9311. www.grousemountain.com.

Aerial tram open year-round daily 9am–10pm; $41.95.
The steep aerial **tram ride** from the base of this attraction rises 1,100m/3,700ft to a ridgeline recreation complex that offers an excellent **panorama★** of the Vancouver area. On clear days, the view embraces Vancouver Island, the Fraser delta and Burrard Inlet. Go to experience the ride and the view from the top, where you can hike, ride a zipline, or have a meal on the outdoor patio of the aging, somewhat run-down lodge. Skiing and snow sports are popular in winter, and **hiking** and **biking** rule in summer. City residents flock here in winter to ski. The **Grouse Grind**, a steep

Indian Arm
For a different type of beach experience, try Indian Arm, the southernmost fjord in North America. This long tongue of saltwater stretches from the east end of Burrard Inlet northward into the heart of the Coast Range. Indian Arm quickly passes from its suburban beginnings into wilderness, with snowcapped peaks above, waterfalls rushing over stone faces, and sandy coves where the dark green water is just warm enough for the adventurous to take a dip. Both canoeing and kayaking are possible in this protected inlet; **Deep Cove Canoe & Kayak Centre** (*2156 Banbury Rd., North Vancouver; 604-929-2268; www.deepcovekayak.com*) offers rentals and guided tours.

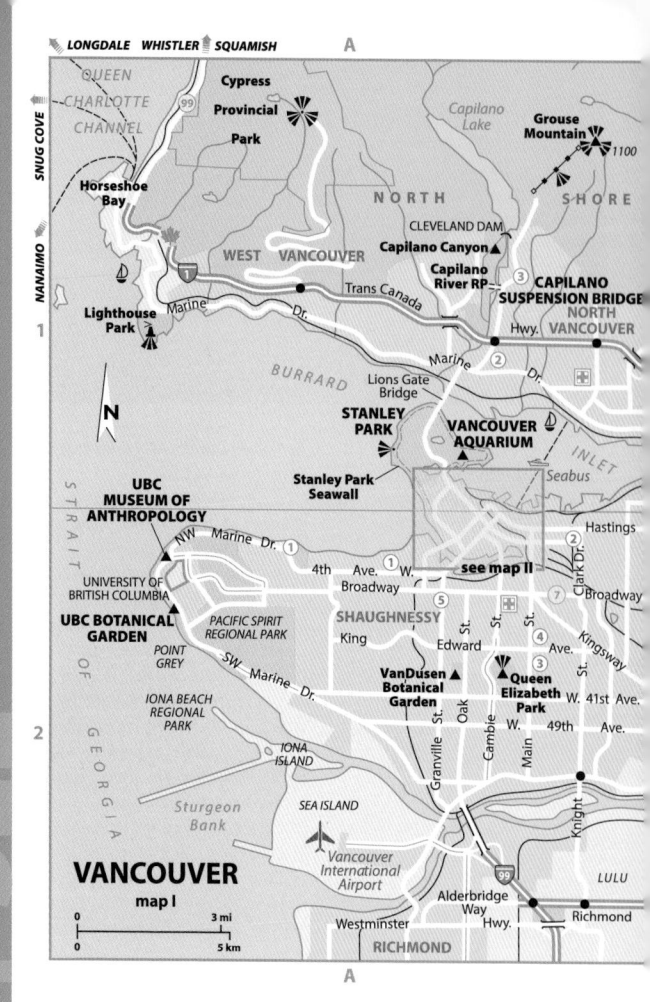

A

QUEEN
CHARLOTTE
CHANNEL

SNUG COVE

NANAIMO

Cypress

Provincial

Park

Horseshoe
Bay

Lighthouse
Park

Capilano
Lake

Grouse
Mountain ⛷1100

N O R T H   S H O R E

CLEVELAND DAM

Capilano Canyon ▲

Capilano
River RP

CAPILANO
SUSPENSION BRIDGE

NORTH
VANCOUVER

WEST VANCOUVER

Trans Canada

Marine   Dr.

Hwy. ②

Marine

Dr.

BURRARD

Lions Gate
Bridge

STANLEY
PARK

VANCOUVER ⚓
AQUARIUM

INLET

Seabus

Stanley Park
Seawall

N

STRAIT

UBC
MUSEUM OF
ANTHROPOLOGY

NW Marine Dr. ①

UNIVERSITY OF
BRITISH COLUMBIA

UBC BOTANICAL
GARDEN

POINT GREY

PACIFIC SPIRIT
REGIONAL PARK

4th   Ave. W.①
Broadway

see map II

Hastings

Clark Dr.

②

⑦ Broadway

SHAUGHNESSY

⑤

King

Edward

IONA BEACH
REGIONAL
PARK

OF

IONA
ISLAND

SEA ISLAND

Sturgeon
Bank

SW Marine Dr.

VanDusen ▲
Botanical
Garden

Queen ⛷
▲Elizabeth
Park

W. 41st Ave.

49th   Ave.

Granville   St.

Oak   St.

Cambie   St.

Main   St.

Knight

GEORGIA

VANCOUVER
map I

0   3 mi

0   5 km

Vancouver
International
Airport

LULU

Alderbridge
Way

Richmond

Westminster

Hwy.

99

RICHMOND

A

climb *(3km/2mi)* that is one of
Vancouver's most popular trails,
ascends the mountain.

Lynn Canyon Park★

*17km/10.5mi north of Vancouver.
Take Hwy. 1 to Lynn Valley Rd.
exit; turn right on Lynn Valley Rd.
and right on Peters Rd. www.
lynncanyon.ca. Open year-round*

*daily 7am; closing hours vary
with the seasons. Ecology Centre
(604-990-3755) open Mon–Fri
10am–5pm, Sat–Sun and holidays
noon–4pm; closed Dec 25–Jan 1.
Suggested donation $2 per person
or $5 per family.*
Lynn Canyon is gem, a small
park that beautifully captures
the finest aspects of the North

HOTELS
Hotelling International
    Jericho Beach...................①
North Vancouver Hotel.......②
Thistledown House..............③

RESTAURANTS
Bishop's.................................①
Pink Pearl.............................②
Sawasdee...............................③
Sun Sui Wah..........................④
Vij's..⑤

MT. SEYMOUR
PROVINCIAL
PARK

Lynn
Canyon
Park

DEEP
COVE

BELCARRA

BELCARRA
REGIONAL
PARK

Dollarton Hwy.

BURRARD INLET

Indian Arm

Ioco
Port Rd.

PORT
MOODY

St.

7A

St. John's St.

SIMON FRASER
UNIVERSITY

BURNABY

COQUITLAM

Como Lake Ave.

MUNDY
PARK

Lougheed Hwy.

Austin Ave.

Burnaby
Lake

MAILLARDVILLE

Burnaby
Village
Museum

BURNABY
LAKE RP

Ave.

Rupert St.

Boundary

NEW
WESTMINSTER

10th

Ave.

H

Fraser River

Marine Way

Fraser River

ISLAND

Fwy.

99A

104th Ave.

GREEN TIMBERS
URBAN FOREST
PARK

WHALLEY

88th Ave.

King George Hwy.

Fraser Hwy.

1A

CHILLIWACK

SURREY

B

Shore: a fast-flowing mountain river, a scary suspension bridge, hushed rain forest pathways, and a friendly and helpful visitor centre. Best of all, the park is a bargain, and is a favoured retreat for in-the-know locals who tend to shun the area's pricier attractions. The 250ha/617acre regional park straddles the canyon of a swift and cold river, **the Lynn**. Trails lead along the canyon rim, through deep forest and into the gorge, where cliff-lined swimming holes await hardy souls. Some 60m/197ft above the forest floor, a short suspension 🚶 **bridge★** straddles the canyon. The **Ecology Centre** features informative exhibits on the park's forests and its denizens.

Capilano River Regional Park

Access from Capilano Rd., just north of the Capilano suspension bridge; and at Cleveland Dam, north end of Capilano Rd. www. metrovancouver.org/services/ parks_lscr/regionalparks/Pages/ CapilanoRiver.aspx.

Encompassing the river's narrow gorge and its hillsides, this park has peaceful 🛶 **hiking trails**, streamside spots for picnicking and contemplation, and scattered patches of old-growth forest. The lower entrance to the park leads to the **Capilano Salmon Hatchery**, where visitors can take a self-guided tour to learn about the life cycle of migrating salmon and steelhead. At the north end of the park, **Cleveland Dam** impounds a drinking-water reservoir, while the top of the dam has excellent **views** of the Lions, the two peaks for which Lions Gate is named.

EAST FRASER VALLEY

Originating in Canada's Rocky Mountains, the **Fraser River** is British Columbia's longest river. The narrow, 145km/90mi expanse of flat river bottom stretching south and east from Vancouver has long been the city's agricultural fringe—and now is its suburban growth area as well. The municipalities of Richmond, Burnaby, Delta, Surrey and New Westminster all have their own city centres, and their own attractions. But they are inarguably satellites to Vancouver, which connects to them via the two Lower Mainland freeways, Highway 99 south to the US border, and Highway 1 (the Trans-Canada Highway) east to Hope.

East of Surrey, development lessens, and the countryside reverts to farmland between Langley and Abbotsford, and on to Chilliwack. The latter community is famed for its **produce stands,** which in late summer offer huge bins of fresh Chilliwack corn.

Burnaby Village Museum★

14km/9mi east of Vancouver via Hastings St. E. east to Hwy. 1; take the Kensington Ave. exit and go south on Kensington Ave.; turn left on Canada Way. 6501 Deer Lake Ave., in Deer Lake Park, Burnaby. 604-297-4565. www.burnabyvillagemuseum.ca. Open May–Sept Tue–Sun 11am– 4:30pm, shorter hours in fall and winter. Dec 13–Jan 2 open daily 1pm-9pm. Closed Dec 24 and 25. Gate admission is free.

Cotton candy spins at a picture show, penny candy fills jars at the **general store**, and the clank of a hammer on hot iron resounds from the **blacksmith shop**.

MUST SEE

Restored 1912 carousel, Burnaby Village Museum

© Burnaby Village Museum

There's a moving picture show, an apothecary and an **ice-cream parlour.** This extensive complex reflects life in the Lower Mainland at the turn of the 19C. Most of the 30-odd restored buildings were moved here from elsewhere. Costumed interpreters on-site offer insights on daily life of a bygone era. A restored 1912 **carousel★★** *(rides $2.50)* delights kids now as much as it did a century ago.

Fort Langley National Historic Site★

56km/35mi southeast of Vancouver via Hwy. 1. Glover St. and Mavis Ave., in Langley. 604-513-4777. www.pc.gc.ca/eng/lhn-nhs/bc/langley/index.aspx. Open year-round daily 10am–5pm. $7.80.
Opened as a Hudson's Bay Company trading post in 1827, this fort played a key role in the settlement of British Columbia for 50 years. Trappers and traders were the first to pass through; then, starting in 1860, gold rushers came here on their way to the Cariboo. British Columbia was declared a British crown colony at the post's

Big House in 1858—an event still commemorated here today. Set on a cottonwood-shaded rise beside the Fraser River, the wooden-palisaded compound includes restored or reconstructed buildings. The **storehouse**, the only structure original to the site, has a fine **collection of furs** and the trading goods once exchanged for them. Costumed interpreters play the part of carpenters, trappers, schoolmarms, barrel-makers, and blacksmiths.

Harrison Hot Springs★

129km/80mi east of Vancouver. Take Hwy. 1 on the south side of the Fraser River to the exit for Agassiz-Harrison (Exit 135) beyond Chilliwack; then Rte. 9 across the river to Kent and continue north on Rte. 9 for 6km/4mi.
This famed resort remains the nearest hot spring to Vancouver and a strong draw for weekend getaways. **Harrison Lake** stretches from here north into the forested vastness of the Coast Range. Set on the south end of the lake (the springs were discovered by

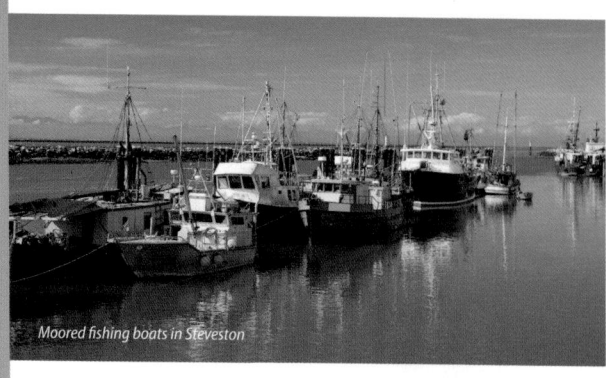
Moored fishing boats in Steveston

© Volodymyr Kyrylyuk / Bigstockphoto.com

boaters who noticed an upwelling of unusually warm water), the resort offers broad sandy beaches that are the site of a celebrated sandcastle competition each September. **Harrison Hot Springs Resort and Spa** *(100 Esplanade; 604-796-2244; www.harrisonresort.com)* draws hot mineral water from underground springs in the lake to fill its soaking pools. You'll also find lodging, dining and spa facilities here.

Hell's Gate Airtram★

52km/32mi north of Hope via Hwy. 1. 604-867-9277. www.hells gateairtram.com. Open mid-Apr– Thanksgiving Monday (second Mon in Oct) daily 10am–4pm. $21.
Fraser Canyon is 180m/600ft deep here, but the rushing river measures only 36m/120ft wide. Early explorer Simon Fraser named this terrifying narrows along the river that bears his name. He wrote in his journal: "We had to travel where no human being should venture—for surely we have encountered the gates of Hell." Once wider, the river was narrowed to its current width by railroad construction in the early

1900s. Through it roars twice as much water as at Niagara Falls. The airtram's gondola descends 152m/500ft from the highway above and crosses the chasm to a landing on the west side, offering a thrilling ride and great views of the narrows.
On the opposite side of the river is a small tourist village with souvenir shops. Visitors can hike down a steep road *(.5km/.3mi)* just south of the airtram parking lot to look at the narrow defile.

Hope★

150km/93mi east of Vancouver via Hwy. 1.
This erstwhile logging town occupies a small pocket along the Fraser River between the Cascade and Coast mountains, and is considered the farthest reach of the Lower Mainland. (Residents of the rest of interior BC refer to the notorious dichotomy in perspective between themselves and Vancouverites by declaring in jest that they live "beyond Hope.") The wildness and unpredictability of the region were well demonstrated by the **Hope Slide** of 1965, when an immense

MUST SEE

amount of rock from Johnson Peak *(18km/11mi east on Hwy. 3)* slid into the valley, filling up a lake. Chainsaw carving is big in these parts; a guide to the two dozen **sculptures** scattered around town is available at the **visitor centre** *(919 Water Ave.; 604-869-2021; www.hopebc.ca).*

FRASER RIVER DELTA

At New Westminster, the Fraser River divides into two major arms, forming a classic fan-shaped delta estuary. Although the flatlands of the delta—its fine soils once were home to numerous farms—are now being converted to suburbs, the area's attractions still derive from its fishing and farming history, and its large population of waterfowl and migratory birds.

George C. Reifel Bird Sanctuary★

32km/20mi south of Vancouver via Hwy. 99 (Exit 28) and Hwy. 17. At Ladner, take Ladner Trunk Rd. west to River Rd. and cross the bridge onto Westham Island. Turn right on Robertson Rd. to the sanctuary. 604-946-6980. www.reifelbirdsanctuary.com. Open year-round daily 9am–4pm. $5. No pets allowed on premises.
Birders take note: this stopover point on the Pacific flyway is one of the most important bird-watching locales in the Vancouver area—more than 260 species have been sighted. Encompassing 300ha/850 acres of wetlands and marsh in the Fraser River Estuary, the sanctuary lands were set aside in the 1960s by George H. Reifel, son of the previous owner, and have since been acquired by the government. During **snow geese** migration

(Nov and Apr), as many as 30,000 of the white geese gather here, creating an unforgettable sight. Rare **tundra swans** have been spotted. Don't forget your binoculars.

Steveston Village★★

27km/17mi south of Vancouver via Hwy. 99 south to Steveston Hwy. (Exit 32); follow Steveston Hwy. west to Fourth Ave. and turn left. www.tourismrichmond.com/ things-to-do/steveston/.
Salt tang flavours the air. The creak of rigging and hulls on dock lofts along the shore. Mist rolls in off the water. You'll savour the atmosphere of a century-old fishing village in this historic complex. Spurred by the restoration of several of its historic sites, the village itself, with its numerous shops and cafes, has become a destination. Fishing isn't dead here; the marina still berths 1,000 boats, including commercial fishers who ply local waters.

Gulf of Georgia Cannery National Historic Site★★

12138 Fourth Ave., Steveston Village. 604-664-9009. http:// www.pc.gc.ca/eng/lhn-nhs/ bc/georgia/index.aspx. Open year-round daily 10am–5pm. $7.80.
The last major cannery on the Fraser River shut down for good in 1979 after almost a century packing salmon, halibut and herring. Now a museum, the complex features a model **canning line** and fascinating exhibits on the heyday of the salmon-packing industry.

EXCURSIONS

The area around Vancouver in British Columbia's southwest corner has some of the most popular travel destinations in North America. Some, such as Victoria, are urban attractions. Others, like Pacific Rim National Park and the Tofino area, rely on their natural beauty to draw visitors. Still others, like Whistler, combine both: spectacular natural features, outdoor recreation and top-notch civilized amenities. To fully appreciate them all would take months, but a one- or two-day side trip to any of them is eminently worthwhile.

VICTORIA★★★

On Vancouver Island. Access from Vancouver via ferry or air only (see Practical Information).

The British Colonial flair that has long characterized Victoria is as evident as ever, but savvy travellers look beyond **afternoon tea** and **horse-drawn carriages** to enjoy the city's beautiful **gardens**, multicultural flavour and outstanding natural setting. Facing the Strait of Juan de Fuca, the city is famous for the mild climate that has made it a **garden capital** and a popular retirement centre as well. Founded in 1843 as a Hudson's Bay Company outpost, and designated the colonial capital in 1862, Victoria was once the next stop on the British Empire circuit after Burma (today's Myanmar) and Hong Kong, from which clipper ships called with tea and other Asian goods. Seat of the provincial government since 1868, Victoria is BC's second-largest metropolitan area, with a population of about 500,000.

🏛 Royal BC Museum★★★

675 Belleville St. 250-356-7226 or 888-447-7977. www.royalbc museum.bc.ca. Open year-round daily 10am–5pm (until 10pm Fri–Sat). IMAX theatre daily

Touring Tip

City centre is situated along **Government Street,** which is the main shopping area, and around the James Bay section of the harbour. Along the harbour **promenade★,** plaques honour clipper ships that once arrived from British Empire outposts. Nearby, shops and cafes border **Bastion Square**. Just north, Victoria's **Chinatown** begins at Herald Street.

10am–8pm. Closed Jan 1 and Dec 25. $23.95, IMAX film $11.95; special exhibits may command a $5 surcharge.

You could easily spend a day at one of Canada's most-visited museums—or on its website, which contains a bounty of detailed information. The Royal BC focuses on the natural and human history of the province, and is most noted for its depiction of First Nations life. Below is an overview of the permanent exhibits.

First Peoples Gallery

The 🏛 **totem poles** on the third floor range from well-weathered historic pieces gathered at coastal villages in the 19C to stunning 20C works carved by artists such

Old Town exhibit, Royal BC Museum

as **Bill Reid** (*see Museums*) and **Mungo Martin**. Faced with the graceful, geometric forms used to represent ravens, bears, eagles, whales and other icons of coastal Native life, the totems exude as much power in the museum halls as they did in seaside villages some 150 years ago.

Two dozen **ceremonial masks**, representing every coastal Native carving style, are stunningly displayed in a dark case where each spotlit mask seems suspended in air. Audio and video presentations depict the ongoing struggle of BC's indigenous peoples to adapt to the modern world, including the restoration of the **potlatch tradition** (during which the masks are used by dancers) that was banned by British authorities in the late 19C. Stroll through the **longhouse** and peer into the **pit house** to gain an appreciation for the lifestyles of the Native American inhabitants.

Modern History Gallery
In this gallery, you can explore 200 years of history, beginning with the days of the European **fur trade** with First Nations inhabitants. Here you can walk the streets of a pioneer **Old Town**; then visit an herbalist shop in a mock **Chinatown**. Finally, clamber around a replica of the *Discovery*, the ship **George Vancouver** sailed into BC waters in the late 18C.

Natural History Gallery
Exceptional **dioramas** in this exhibit space illustrate the province's varied **ecosystems,** from temperate rain forest to interior desert.

The museum is also a prominent stopping point for international exhibits, such as Egyptian antiquities, that sometimes visit no other North American venues. The lobby of the **museum's archives** now holds a rotating display of historic documents, diaries and photographs.

Thunderbird Park
Adjacent to the museum at Belleville and Douglas Sts. This park has an wealth of fine **totem poles★★** from many First Nations groups, allowing visitors to appreciate the different carving styles.

BUTCHART GARDENS

VICTORIA

CHINATOWN

Fisgard   St.

CENTENNIAL
SQUARE

MARKET
SQUARE

Pandora

0   250 m

0   1/8 mi

Johnson St.
Bridge

Johnson

OLD TOWN

BASTION
SQUARE

**Maritime Museum
of British Columbia**

Yates   St.

St.

Inner

View   St.

Wharf   Fort
Street   St.

Broughton

Harbour

Courtney   St.

Humboldt

Blanshard

Fort   St.

Douglas

Quadra

PIONEER
SQUARE

James Bay

Government

Burdett Ave.

CHRIST CHURCH
CATHEDRAL

**Empress
Hotel**

CONF.
CENTRE

Belleville

Belleville St.

Fairfield

McClure St.

NETHERLANDS
CARILLON TOWER

Government

Thunderbird Park
**Helmcken
House**

ST. ANN'S
ACADEMY

Humboldt

Vancouver

**ROYAL BC
MUSEUM**

**Parliament
Buildings**

Douglas
St.

Quadra

Menzies

Superior   St.

Michigan   St.

**Beacon Hill
Park**

SCENIC MARINE DRIVE

CRAIGDARROCH CASTLE

GOVERNMENT HOUSE

HOTELS	
Bedford Regency	①
Fairholme Manor	②
The Fairmont Empress	③
Haterleigh Heritage Inn	④
Magnolia Hotel & Spa	⑤
Rosewood Victoria Inn	⑥

RESTAURANTS	
Bengal Lounge	①
Blue Fox	②
Café Brio	③
Ming's	④
Spinnaker's Gastro Brewpub	⑤
Ulla	⑥

Helmcken House★
675 Belleville St. 250-356-7226
www.royalbcmuseum.bc.ca.
Open for special events; call or
check online.
This restored 1852 house, located
behind the Royal BC Museum,
was home to a physician to the
Hudson's Bay Company at Fort
Victoria. He and his wife raised
their seven children here. Rooms

are decorated in period furnishings
brought around Cape Horn on
clipper ships to Victoria.

Empress Hotel★★
721 Government St.
250-384-8111 or 866-540-4429.
www.fairmont.com/empress.
Ah, the Empress, symbol of
gentility. Designed by famed
colonial architect Francis

Rattenbury, this massive neo-Gothic granite landmark anchors Victoria's Inner Harbour. Since its 1908 opening, the Empress has epitomized the civility of the empire whose last days it witnessed. Over the years, this grande dame of hospitality has hosted royalty, celebrities, elite travellers and countless honeymooners. The hotel's public spaces include a vast **Edwardian lobby**; the glass-ceilinged Victorian **Palm Court**; the Crystal Ballroom; several clubby, dark-wood restaurants, lounges and sitting rooms; Willow Stream Spa; and the **Bengal Lounge**, whose colonial artifacts include tiger skins given to the hotel by the Thai royal family when they visited in the 1930s. Built by Canadian Pacific Railway as the westernmost property in its continent-wide chain of château hotels, the Empress is now operated by the Fairmont group (*see Hotels*).

The Cougar Incident

As if to prove conclusively that no amount of civilizing can utterly tame Vancouver Island, one of the wildest of island creatures, a cougar, was discovered in the heart of Victorian urbanity—the Empress Hotel parking garage—in 1992. The garage gates were closed, wildlife officials called, and the cougar was tranquilized and returned to the wild. Victoria author Julie Lawson used the incident as the basis for a popular children's book, *In Like a Lion*—copies are, of course, available at the Empress news shop. Vancouver Island is considered by some wildlife experts to have the greatest density of mountain lions on earth.

Parliament Buildings★

501 Belleville St. 250-387-3046. www.leg.bc.ca. Open mid-May–Labour Day daily 9am–5pm. Rest of the year Mon–Fri 9am–5pm. Intended to reflect the character, if not the actual majesty, of London's Parliament, this complex was designed by **Francis Rattenbury** *(see sidebar below)*, architect of the Empress Hotel. He blended (critics say he "mashed together") Victorian, Romanesque and Italianate design elements, including 33 copper domes, to create a complex that is one of Victoria's visual icons. The BC Legislature is in session here in winter and spring; **guided tours** *(45min)* explain the sometimes

---

🍵 Tea at the Empress

Victorian matrons, no doubt smartly attired, were the first patrons when the Empress began its famous tea service back in 1908. Today both the dress code and the service have become less formal (no shorts though, please), but the atmosphere remains largely the same. Served in the hotel's elegant, high-ceilinged lobby, or in the Palm Court, afternoon tea is offered at five sittings a day. Traditional finger sandwiches, scones, crumpets, pastries, heavy cream and seasonal berry preserves are presented, along with the Empress' own proprietary tea blend. It's not cheap—figure up to $60 a person (varies by season). Reservations are essential: *250-389-2727.*

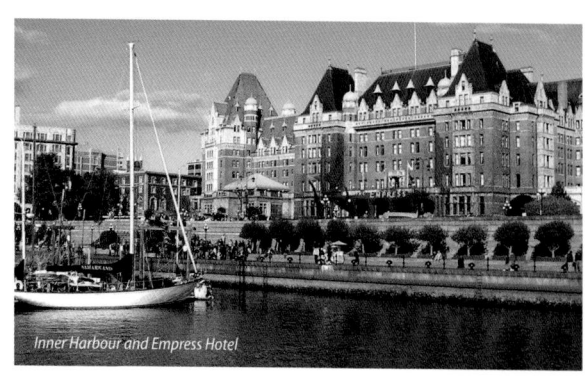

Inner Harbour and Empress Hotel

© Leslie Forsberg / Michelin

inexplicable workings of BC government, as well as the building's history. And what would a building of British heritage be without **statues**? An image of Queen Victoria stands out front, and Captain George Vancouver's likeness tops the highest dome.

Government Street★

Victoria's principal thoroughfare in Old Town is also its main shopping street, with venerable stores that are destinations in themselves. Here's a selection. Be sure to poke your head in at least one of them.
♦ **Rogers Chocolates** (*no. 913; 250-881-8771; www.rogers chocolates.com*) occupies a 1903 building with tile floors and oak display cases. The company began making its classic British-style truffles and candies in 1885. "Victoria creams" are Rogers' signature confection. They are definitely hard to resist.
♦ **Murchie's Teas** (*no. 1110; 250-383-3112; www.murchies.com*) dates its business back to colonial days, when clipper ships called from Hong Kong with tea bales on board. (Remember all the trouble that caused in Boston?) Like its counterpart branch in Vancouver, teas here range from everyday orange pekoe to $99-an-ounce handpicked blends that, believe it or not, are good enough to justify the cost.

Francis Rattenbury

Francis Mawson Rattenbury (1867–1935) lived a life as colourful as his famous designs are grandiose. Born in England, he achieved modest success as an architect until he moved to British Columbia, and wangled the commission to design Victoria's Parliament Buildings in the late 1890s. That got him hired by Canadian Pacific folks, who set him to work designing the Empress Hotel. Rattenbury cut quite a figure in BC society, until the revelation of an affair with Alma Pakenham, who was 30 years his junior, drove both from the New World back to the Old. There Rattenbury was murdered; Alma and her new lover were charged. He was sentenced to life in prison, and she committed suicide.

- **Munro's Books** (*no. 1108; 250-382-2464; www.munrobooks.com*) sits next door to Murchie's in an elegant late-19C bank building, with high, pressed-tin ceilings. Munro's selection of BC books is superlative. Jim Munro, the founder and owner, was the husband of world-famous author, Alice Munro. The store celebrates its 50th anniversary in 2013.

- **Old Morris Tobacconist** (*no. 1116; 250-382-4811; www.oldmorris.com*) has a heady array of pipe tobaccos, which, signifying the store's British leanings, are stored in the humidor. The cigars are out in the open, and yes, Cuban cigars number among the selection.

Maritime Museum of British Columbia★

28 Bastion Square. 250-385-4222. www.mmbc.bc.ca. Open year-round daily 10am–5pm (Thu–Sat until 9pm). $12.

You'll recognize this building by the **lighthouse beacon** outside it. Housed in the old courthouse, the maritime museum presents an eclectic collection of maps, artifacts, charts and model ships that depicts the province's seafaring past. Two small boats—a traditional **dugout canoe** and a **ketch**—offer up-close evidence of the adventurous spirit of the early mariners.

Inner Harbour
Along Wharf St.

The heart of Victoria edges this lively, boat and floatplane-filled harbour, with the Empress Hotel directly ahead, the Parliament Buildings to one side, and Old Town to the other. Here, on a summer day, fresh breezes blow off the water, street musicians ply their craft on stone benches, hanging baskets of petunias and geraniums glisten in the sun, and you could almost swear it was the year 1900.

Tourism Victoria's main visitor centre is located at the west end of the Inner Harbour (*812 Wharf St.; 250-953-2033 or 800-663-3883; www.tourismvictoria.com; open May–Sep daily 8:30am–7:30pm, rest of the year daily 9am–5pm; closed Dec 25*).

EXCURSIONS

Chinatown

Bounded by Pandora Ave., Herald, Government and Store Sts.

Encompassing two city blocks, Victoria's Chinatown, though much smaller in scale than Vancouver's, has some of the same flavour—tea, herb and spice shops; stalls with exotic produce; Asian imports stores; and dim sum restaurants. The entrance to Chinatown is marked by the 1981 **Gate of Harmonious Interest★**, a lavishly figured, vividly coloured archway over Fisgard Street at Government. The adjoining **Fan Tan Alley**, just .9m/3ft wide at its narrowest, and reputedly Canada's narrowest alley, is a warren of small shops. Once this district harboured gambling and opium dens.

Silk Road Tea

1624 Government St. 250-704-2688. www.silkroadtea.com. This superlative tea and bath shop in Chinatown proffers bath salts and soaps with exotic herbs and oils.

🦆 Scenic Marine Drive★★

Begin at Thunderbird Park, Douglas and Belleville Sts.

This drive reveals Victoria's splendid setting on the **Strait of Juan de Fuca**, yielding views of the city's gardens, neighbourhoods and scenic vistas. Start at Thunderbird Park, and head south on Douglas Street, past Beacon Hill Park and a plaque noting the starting point of Highway 1, the Trans-Canada Highway. Turn left on Dallas Road, heading east along the water. At Finlayson and Cover Points, enjoy **panoramic views** of the strait, with the Olympic Mountains in Washington State in the distance.

Craigdarroch Castle

© Bruce Davies / Craigdarroch Castle

Craigdarroch Castle★

1050 Joan Crescent. 250-592-5323. www.thecastle.ca. Open mid-Jun–Labour Day daily 9am–7pm, rest of year daily 10am–4:30pm. Closed Jan 1 and Dec 25–26. $13.95.

Scottish immigrant **Robert Dunsmuir** was BC's first tycoon, a coal baron who meant this castle to be the most grandiose home on North America's Pacific coast. The mansion was finished in the late 1890s but, in an irony of biblical proportions, Dunsmuir was never able to glory in his creation—he died before it was done. The four-storey sandstone, granite and marble structure, complete with turrets and towers, shelters an opulent interior. Inside, meticulously hand-carved walls and intricate ceiling panelling greet visitors. Numerous ceiling-high **stained-glass panels** outshine all but the world's biggest cathedrals. The 87 steps of the massive oak stairway lead to a fourth-floor **ballroom**.

🦆 Butchart Gardens★★★

North of Victoria, in Brentwood Bay. Take Hwy. 17 to Keating Cross Rd. 250-652-4422 or 866-652-4422. www.butchartgardens.com. Open year-round daily 9am–dusk (opens at 1pm Dec 25). Rates are

seasonal, ranging from $17.40 in winter, to $30.80 in summer.
When you see these spectacular gardens, you'll be hard-pressed to imagine that this site was once a gaping quarry. In 1904 Jennie Butchart had a vision for the operations. The 20ha/50 acres of gardens that resulted have achieved world fame for their splendour and variety. Still run by the Butchart family and headed by Jennie's great-granddaughter, the gardens are among Canada's most popular attractions.

Sunken Garden
The justly famed and oft-pictured heart of the old quarry is the **centrepiece garden**. Green lawns curve around carefully tended masses of bright annuals, perennials and bulbs. The displays change with the season, and even winter has its blooms.

Ross Fountain
Within a rocky pool at the south end of the Sunken Garden, dramatic **water displays** feature changing patterns and, at night, an array of coloured lights.

Rose Garden
This popular plot holds a maze of bloom-covered arbors in peak season *(Jun–Sept)*, attracting rose lovers from around the world.

Japanese Garden
A secluded spot, the garden features exquisite lacquered **bridges** and wooden **teahouses**.

Italian Garden
This formal garden has **statuary** and a star-shaped **lily pond** surrounded by colourful plantings.

Touring Tip

Butchart's popularity has its drawbacks: peak summer days can find more than 50 tour buses in the huge parking lot, and the crowded paths can dampen your experience somewhat. Garden managers do what they can to minimize the effects of crowding (smoking is forbidden, for instance), but it's best to arrive early, or visit in spring and fall. In summer however, a **fireworks display** lights up the sky on Saturday nights. For a small re-admission fee *($3.50)* you can return the following day, provided it's not a special events day, to spread your visit over two days. The on-site store sells a vast array of books devoted to gardening, botany and horticulture, as well as souvenirs and gift items. There is a restaurant on the premises.

Fort Rodd Hill National Historic Site★★
603 Fort Rodd Hill Rd. 14km/9mi west of Victoria via Rtes. 1, 1A and Ocean Blvd. 250-478-5849.www. fortroddhill.com. Open mid-Feb–Oct daily 10am–5:30pm. Rest of the year daily 9am–4:30pm. Closed Dec 25 and 26, and Jan 1. $4.
Set on 18ha/44 acres of land at the southwest corner of Esquimalt's harbour, this fort defended Victoria and the nearby Esquimalt naval base from 1878 until 1956. Today the ruins of three coastal artillery **gun batteries** remain to tell the tale. Wander through the guardhouses, barracks and magazines to get a feel for day-to-day life in the garrison long ago. Built in 1860, **Fisgard Lighthouse**

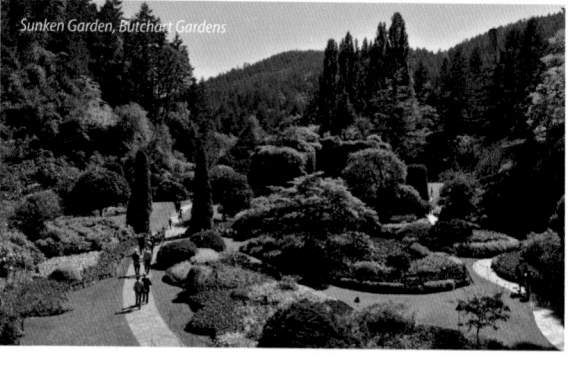
Sunken Garden, Butchart Gardens

© Courtesy of The Butchart Gardens

was the first permanent light on the west coast of Canada; the house where the light's keeper once lived now contains exhibits and videos relating to the site. Here you'll also enjoy great **views★** of Juan de Fuca Strait and the Olympic Mountains. **Langley Centennial Museum** *(see Museums)* is located nearby.

🍁 PACIFIC RIM NATIONAL PARK RESERVE★★★

Take Hwy. 1 north from Victoria to Parksville, then take Hwy. 4 west, through Port Alberni to the park. 250-726-7721 www.pc.gc. ca/eng/pn-np/bc/pacificrim/index. aspx. Open daily year-round; park facilities closed mid-Oct–mid-Mar. $7.80.

Wave-tossed rocky headlands, long sandy beaches, old-growth spruce forests and an inland sound with untouched islands are some of the natural elements that make up this outstanding natural preserve. Hugging the west coast of Vancouver Island, the National Park includes three distinct units: Long Beach, Broken Group Islands and West Coast Trail. The park's **visitor centre** *(open mid-Mar–mid-Oct daily 10am–4:30pm; 250-726-4600)* is located just past the junction where Highway 4 turns north.

Long Beach★★

Stretching from just north of Ucluelet in the south, where Highway 4 turns north, northward to within 4.8km/3mi of Tofino, this area is the only part of the park reachable by a road. The namesake beach has almost 32km/20mi of shoreline, most of it open beach, with firm gray sand for strolling, offshore **sea stacks** to send waves crashing upward, and open expanses where the perfect curls of breaking waves draw dozens of **surfers** (Tofino is widely regarded as the surfing capital of Canada).

Radar Hill★★

About 29km/18mi north of the visitor centre, the 91m/300ft summit (highest on this stretch of coast) of this hill affords a 360-degree **panorama★★** of the ocean and the island behind. The road ends in **Tofino★**, 33.5km/21mi northwest of the Ucluelet junction.

Broken Group Islands

The second unit, composed of more than 100 islands, is contained entirely within **Barkley Sound,** a small inland sound south of Ucluelet. It is one of the premier saltwater **kayaking** areas on earth. Permits are required to visit the islands; outfitting and transport to the sound are available in Ucluelet.

West Coast Trail

This legendary 75km/47mi wilderness trail traverses the coast between Bamfield and Port Renfrew, a unique and beautiful trek that takes up to seven days. The trail lures hikers from around the world, who are attracted by its wonderful shoreline trails, seaside campfires, towering untouched forests, hair-raising ladders and suspension bridges, cable car crossings over icy mountain streams, tidal pools rich with sea life, and frequent sightings of orcas, dolphins, and gray whales. Reservations are necessary in advance, as park officials limit its use to about 70 people per day, but are easy to make on the national park website.

Salmon Fishing

Wild BC salmon is regarded as the most delicious (and healthy!) in the world. Rivers are abundant with salmon, and Vancouver Island has its share. **Big Bear Salmon Charters**, based in Ucluelet, offers salmon fishing tours for anyone interested in catching their own dinner. Guided tours and equipment, plus instruction, are provided. *www. bigbearsalmoncharters.com or 855-972-5666.*

Kwisitis (Wickaninnish) Visitor Centre

At end of Wick Rd., 8km/5mi north of the main park visitor centre. www.pc.gc.ca. Open May –mid-Oct daily. 10am–4:30pm.

This interpretive facility explains the North Pacific ecosystem, including the life cycles of the **gray whales** that pass just offshore during their annual migration between Alaska and Mexico.

Long Beach, Pacific Rim National Park Reserve

© Deddeda / age fotostock

NEAR THE PARK

🛁 Hot Springs Cove★

North of Tofino; access by boat only. Charters leave Tofino year-round.

Few places anywhere on earth offer what this legendary **provincial park** does: an unparalleled sensory experience for bathers. The hot spring waters arise in a headland about 61m/200ft inland and spill down the rocky channel to the Pacific waters of Clayoquot Sound. You can sit in the **hot-water pools** and let the cold seawater wash over you as waves arrive. The view out over the ocean, the salt breeze, and the peaceful wilderness surroundings all combine to make one of the most memorable experiences of a lifetime.

It's best to come here during the week in spring and fall, when crowds are low. Along the way, you might see whales, dolphins, sea lions and eagles. **Jamie's Whaling Station** is the leading tour operator in Tofino *(606 Campbell St.; 250-725-3919 or 800-667-9913; www.jamies.com).*

Tofino★

At the end of northern end of Hwy. 4, on Long Beach peninsula. www.tofino-bc.com.

This small harbour receives more than one million visitors in summer. Erstwhile logging and fishing capital, Tofino is popular as a **surfing centre**. The community's central role in the Clayoquot Sound logging furor has brought it a distinct countercultural flavour. You'll often see barefooted youths traipsing through town with hefty packs, just as you'll see pickup trucks piled high with fishing nets, and family vans with tourists. Tofino hardly attracted anyone in winter until the opening of Wickaninnish Inn *(see Hotels)* kicked off the storm-watching aspect of the coastal visitor industry. Whale-watching, surfing, national-park camping, upscale accommodations, commercial fishing, and holdover logging—it's a heady cultural mix in this little town, and that's part of its unique character.

Clayoquot Sound

Pocked by dozens of small islands, this vast body of in-shore saltwater northeast of Tofino has a fascinating modern cultural history. Settlement on the sound began with a Nootka band under the leadership of Chief Wickaninnish. In the 20C, plans to turn the sound's forests over to timber companies for clear-cutting provoked an international outcry that attracted protestors from around the world, especially Europe. At one point, demonstrators seized the bridge over the Kennedy River and blocked traffic on Highway 4 for two days. The uproar eventually forced the provincial government to back down, and all interested parties—timber companies, environmental activists, First Nations bands and local residents—hammered out an agreement that allows limited selective logging in the area, but not clear-cutting. The whole story, along with the delicate balance of life in the rain forest ecosystem, is told at the **Rainforest Interpretive Centre** in Tofino *(451 Main St.; 250-725-2560, www.raincoasteducation.org).*

♦ **Hanging Garden Tree** –
Along the main hiking path on Meares Island, just east of Tofino in Clayoquot Sound. Access by water taxi from Tofino.

Here's a natural sight that's worth a 20min hike: the 1,000-year-old Hanging Garden Tree. This much-photographed **Western red cedar** has been worn down over time into a bulky 30m/100ft vertical burl with numerous side-limbs and a base broad enough to anchor a suspension bridge. The cracks and shoulders along the trunk have accumulated debris, which decayed into soil and sprouted wind-blown seeds.

The Hanging Garden Tree became a visual symbol for the early 1990s campaign to protect the sound's forest from clear-cutting. The controversy has muted now, and the tree remains—a host to dozens of other growing things.

MORE MUST SEES ON VANCOUVER ISLAND

Cathedral Grove★★
Along Hwy. 4, about 16 km/ 10mi west of Parksville. www.cathedralgrove.eu.

One of the last remaining **old-growth groves** on lower Vancouver Island was given to the province by lumber baron H.R. MacMillan. The Douglas firs in this magnificent grove approach 75m/250ft in height and 1,000 years in age. Short 🚶 **hiking trails** lead from the highway (which splits the grove) into the woods; an elevated walkway affords a good **view** of the devastation caused by a fierce windstorm in the mid-1990s.

Cowichan Valley★
On Hwy. 1, about 80km/50mi north of Victoria.

As Highway 1 leaves Victoria, it climbs a steep grade called **Malahat Mountain**, atop which viewpoints afford sensational **views** of the Gulf Islands and San Juan Islands, with the US mainland's snowcapped Mount Baker in the distance. The road then descends to sea level, entering the valley of the **Cowichan River.** The name is a translation of a Native word that means "warm land," a reflection of the area's benign climate. That climate has led to the development of a nascent **wine-growing district**. Most of the vineyards are fairly young, and viticulturists and winemakers are still learning the eccentricities of their climate (it may be warm, but it's not California). The area's road network is a farm-country maze, so it's best to phone for directions to the following wineries:

♦ **Vigneti Zanatta** *(5039 Marshall Rd., Duncan; 250-748-2338; www. zanatta.ca)*, oldest in the district, it also has Vinoteca, a fine restaurant and wine bar in a heritage farm-house *(open for lunch Wed–Sun).*

♦ **Cherry Point Vineyards** *(840 Cherry Point Rd., Cobble Hill; 250-743-1272; cherrypointestate wines.com)* has a tasting room that is open daily.

♦ **Blue Grouse Vineyards** *(4365 Blue Grouse Rd., Duncan; 250-743-3834; www.bluegrousevineyards. com)* is a family-run winery with a tasting room open four days a week.

♦ **Merridale Cidery** *(1230 Merridale Rd., Cobble Hill; 250-743-4293 or 1-800-998-9908; www.merridalecider.com)* is the leading West Coast orchard, with

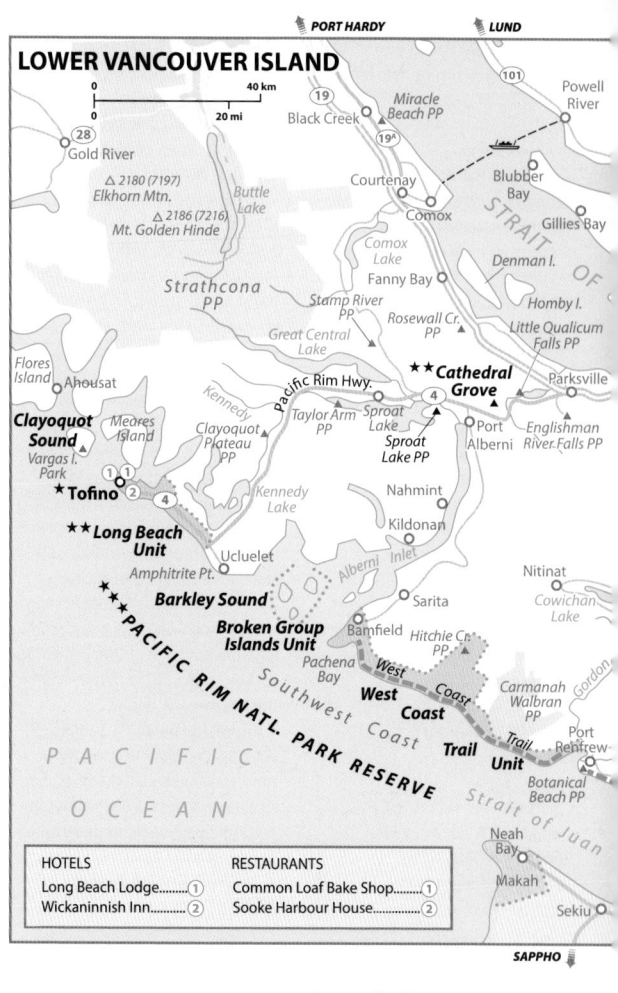

LOWER VANCOUVER ISLAND

▲ PORT HARDY   ▲ LUND

Powell River

⊙28 Gold River

△ 2180 (7197) Elkhorn Mtn.
△ 2186 (7216) Mt. Golden Hinde

Buttle Lake

Strathcona PP

Black Creek

Miracle Beach PP

19A

Courtenay

Comox

Comox Lake

Fanny Bay

Stamp River PP

Great Central Lake

Blubber Bay

Gillies Bay

STRAIT OF

Denman I.

Homby I.

Little Qualicum Falls PP

Rosewall Cr. PP

Flores Island ⊙Ahousat

Kennedy R.

Pacific Rim Hwy.

Taylor Arm PP

Sproat Lake

★★ Cathedral Grove

Parksville

Clayoquot Sound

Meares Island

Clayoquot Plateau PP

Vargas I. Park

1 1
2
4

Kennedy Lake

★ **Tofino**

Sproat Lake PP

Port Alberni

Englishman River Falls PP

Nahmint

Kildonan

★★ **Long Beach Unit**

Ucluelet

Amphitrite Pt.

Alberni Inlet

Sarita

Nitinat

Cowichan Lake

★★ **Barkley Sound**

Broken Group Islands Unit

Bamfield

Hitchie Cr. PP

Pachena Bay

West Coast

Carmanah Walbran PP

Gordon R.

★★★ **PACIFIC RIM NATL. PARK RESERVE**

Southwest Coast

West Coast Trail Unit

Port Renfrew

Botanical Beach PP

P A C I F I C

O C E A N

Strait of Juan

Neah Bay

Makah

Sekiu ⊙

SAPPHO

HOTELS	RESTAURANTS
Long Beach Lodge.........①	Common Loaf Bake Shop.........①
Wickaninnish Inn...........②	Sooke Harbour House...............②

0   40 km
0   20 mi

101

more than 4ha/10 acres planted with hundreds of apple trees—they pioneered hard-cider making in the West. Visitors are welcome year-round *(call for hours)*, but the best time to stop by is September and October, when daily pressings produce gallons upon gallons of highly flavoured juice.

Juan de Fuca Provincial Park

On Hwy. 14, west of Sooke. 250-474-1336. www.env.gov.bc.ca/ bcparks. Open year-round daily dawn–dusk.

This shoreline preserve hugs the coast south of Port Renfrew—in some places stretching less than half a kilometre (.25mi) inland from

WHISTLER

★★ **Sea to Sky Highway**

Garibaldi
PP

Harmony
Islands
MP

Jervis
Inlet

99

▲ Alice Lake PP

Saltery Bay
Earls Cove

Cheekye

Saltery
Bay
PP

▲ Skookumchuk
Narrows PP

Tantalus PP

Squamish

○ Squamish

Texada
Island

Madeira
Park

Porteau Cove PP ▲

Pinecone-
Burke PP

Jedediah Islands
▲ MP

Porpoise Bay
PP

Sechelt

Gambier
Island

99

Mt. Seymour
PP

Roberts Cr.
PP

Gibsons

Lions Bay

Indian
Arm PP

Pitt
Lake

GEORGIA

Horseshoe
Bay

Southeast Coast

★★★ **VANCOUVER**

7

Coquitlam

Gabriola

Richmond

99

Surrey

HOPE

Nanaimo

1

Valdes I.

Tsawwassen

Blaine

Dionisio
Point MP

Ladysmith

Gulf Islands

Galiano
I.

Montague
Harbour MP

Birch Bay SP ▲

Ferndale

5

SEATTLE

Chemainus

Youbou
Lake
Cowichan

Ganges

Mayne I.

Lummi

Gordon
Bay PP

★ **Cowichan**
Valley

18

Cowichan
River PP

Duncan

Winter Cove PMP
Saturna I.

Bellingham

San Juan

Salt Spring
Island

San Juan
Islands

Shawnigan
Lake

Sidney

17

Anacortes

14

Juan de Fuca
Trail

★★ **Fort**
Rodd Hill

★★ **Juan de**
Fuca PP

River Jordan

14

2

Esquimalt

☆

Fisgard
Lighthouse

★★★ **BUTCHART**
GARDENS

17A

★★★ **VICTORIA**

20

French Beach
PP

Sooke

East Sooke
RP

Swinomish

de Fuca

Clallam
Bay

Oak Harbor

PORT ANGELES   PORT ANGELES   SEATTLE

the beach. A multifaceted wonder, the park offers different levels of experience of the West Coast of Vancouver Island. Four access points allow **easy hikes** down to the shore, where Pacific breakers roll in on pebble-sand beaches; trails descend through old-growth Sitka spruce, massive trees with gnarled branches that can tolerate salt spray, and thrive on headlands and coastal sites. **China Beach**, the first access, and **Botanical Beach**, the most distant *(2.5hrs from Victoria)* are the best beaches. At the latter, low tide reveals **tide pools** with anemones, crabs, shellfish and nudibranchs, and starfish on the rocks.

WHISTLER★★★

Take Hwy. 1 in West Vancouver west to Horseshoe Bay, then follow Hwy. 99 north about 102km/63mi. Tourist information: Whistler Visitor Centre, 4230 Gateway Dr.; 604-935-3357 or 877-991-9988; www.whistler.com/whistler-visitor-centre.

Less than 50 years old, Whistler today is one of the largest and most popular ski resorts in the world. Nonetheless it confines itself to a relatively compact developed area in a bowl-shaped valley deep within the Coast Range. The community has adopted a "bed cap" that limits residential and hospitality growth, since this year-round resort attracts visitors in all seasons.

If You Don't Ski
Fabulous restaurants, shops, spas and nightclubs await you 12 months a year. 🥾 **Hiking**, biking, golf, canoeing, rafting, ballooning, fishing, climbing and horse riding fill the **summer**; in **winter**, go 🏒 **ice skating**, dog-sledding, tubing, Nordic skiing and snowmobiling.

🎿 If You Do Ski
Two mountains that, combined, appear at the top of most ski resort ratings every year. No other area in North America has as great a **vertical drop**—1,609m/5,280ft. No other area has as long a season—skiing continues on the Blackcomb Glacier until August *(see sidebar below; www.whistlerblackcomb.com)*. Whistler advertises itself as a full-service resort; buy a ski/golf package to ski in the morning, and swing a golf club in the afternoon!

Whistler in Summer
In summer the area's setting and character draw large numbers of visitors for numerous outdoor activities.

♦ **Mountain Peeking** – Try the view from above. Take the **Whistler Gondola** *(open late Jun–late Sept daily 10am–4pm)* for a ride

Biking at Whistler

© Tourism Whistler / Mike Crane

Winter Olympics 2010

Whistler's founders in the early 1960s dreamed that one day the area would host a Winter Olympics. The fantasy came true in July 2003 when, in tandem with Vancouver, the 2010 winter games were awarded to the region. Among the area's virtues that appealed to the International Olympic committee is the fact that Whistler can handle an event of such global proportions with relatively modest preparation. Alpine events—downhill skiing, bobsledding, ski jumping—took place on Whistler and Blackcomb mountains. A bobsled and luge facility was built, but existing lifts and other facilities were sufficiently adequate. A Nordic ski centre was built in a nearby valley, adding to Whistler's overall appeal for years to come.

MUST SEE

Skiing Whistler and Blackcomb

The season runs roughly November to April. Of the 37 lifts, 14 high-speed lifts can carry 52,000 skiers an hour to the top of Blackcomb Mountain and Whistler Mountain, two nearly identical peaks that face each other across a small valley. Annual snowfall averages 9m/30ft, and since the valley is clasped within the middle of the Coast Range 80km/50mi from Howe Sound, the snow is not as wet and heavy as at Northwest resorts directly facing the ocean. There are 200 trails, 12 bowls and three glaciers in 2,833ha/7,000 acres of ski-able terrain—the longest intermediate run stretches a luxurious 11km/7mi. The base is at 670.5m/2,200ft, and skiing tops out at about 2,286m/7,500ft on both mountains. One lift ticket covers both: *$98 in high season.*

to the top ($52.95); you can even include a barbecue lunch at the mountaintop restaurant.

♦ **Biking** – Energetic visitors rent mountain bikes at the **Garbanzo Bike & Bean Shop** *(at the foot of the lift; 604-905-2076; www.whistlerbike.com)* and ride all the way down Whistler—the descent takes about three hours. Ride or bike down—you'll enjoy magnificent panoramas of numerous **Coast Range** peaks in every direction.

♦ **Canoeing and River Running** – **Whistler Outdoor Experience** *(604-932-3389)* rents equipment and provides guided tours for canoe trips on clear, cold **Green Lake** *(8km/5mi east of Whistler Village)*, and sponsors guided **kayak** and canoe trips down the **River of Golden Dreams**.

♦ **Golf** – **The Château Whistler Golf Club** *(604-938-2092; www.fairmontgolf.com/whistler)* was designed by Robert Trent Jones, Jr.; the 122m/400ft elevation gain along the course is softened by the GPS computers onboard the carts. **Nicklaus North** *(604-896-2224; www.golfbc.com/courses/furry_creek)*, designed by Jack Nicklaus, winds around Green Lake.

♦ **Fishing** – The streams and rivers

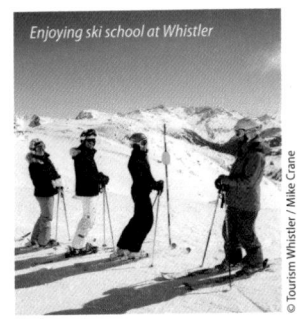
Enjoying ski school at Whistler

© Tourism Whistler / Mike Crane

around Whistler are rich with game fish like salmon, steelhead, trout and char, and opportunities abound for **backcountry fishing** adventures. **Whistler Flyfishing**, long-established and with a great reputation, offers the complete package: an online store, two outfitting shops (one in Whistler and one in Squamish), guiding angling tours all year-round, and even a fly-fishing academy for those who want to learn how to do it right! *www.whistlerflyfishing.com or 888-822-3474.*

🐟 OKANAGAN VALLEY★★

From Vancouver, follow Hwy. 1 east, then take Hwy. 5 (the Coquihalla Hwy.) northeast, then take Hwy. 97C and Hwy. 97 east to Kelowna.

Whale Watching off Vancouver Island

The whales that ply the inland and coastal waters of the Pacific Northwest are among North America's most beloved wild creatures. Thousands of sightseers board boats daily to head out in hopes of a glimpse of graceful black-and-white **orcas** slipping through the Georgia Strait, or the much bigger **gray whales** that migrate north and south along the Pacific coast between Alaska and Mexico. These cruises are among the most popular of visitor activities, but controversy accompanies them. Some conservation advocates (and some scientists) believe the unremitting presence of dozens of noisy boats interferes with the whales' daily lives, especially the orcas, who use sound waves to communicate and to locate prey.

The Puget Sound killer-whale pods, in particular, may be in decline, though scientists debate the reasons. You can see whales from many shoreline points, such as those in Victoria's Oak Bay neighbourhood, though sightings cannot be guaranteed. Be sure the boat you board subscribes to the industry's code of ethics, which forbids chasing whales, and prescribes a minimum distance between boats and whales.

For referrals to whale-watching companies that adhere to the code of ethics, contact **Victoria Tourism** (*250-953-2033 or 800-663-3883; www. tourismvictoria.com*). For information about whale-watching cruises from Vancouver, *see Outdoor Fun.*

Clasped between towering highlands on either side, the Okanagan Valley runs north-south along its namesake lake and river—a geographic happenstance that has resulted in a sun-rich climate perfect for growing **fruits and vegetables** (an industry that dates back to the mid-19C). The climate is also perfect for growing retirement communities. Modern development of subdivisions, golf courses and shopping centres has begun to threaten the viability of the region's longstanding agricultural community.

Okanagan Lake★★

Monsters unknown to science ply the 305m/1,000ft deep waters of this 121km/75mi-long spring-fed lake. So goes the legend, anyway; local officials have periodically offered a million-dollar reward to anyone who acquires incontrovertible proof that **Ogopogo** actually exists. So far, the closest claimant turned out to be a video of an extra-large beaver. The lake is a geographic and recreational marvel—it never freezes; it has so far withstood the pollution of urban development; and it hardly ever varies much in depth, though its lower end has just a modest weir leading to its outflow. Boaters, canoeists, sailors, anglers, sailboarders and swimmers all enjoy its waters, as do countless waterfowl.

When you come down from the Okanagan Highlands on Highway 97C, the first sight of the sparkling blue lake is one of the more memorable vistas in BC. Ogopogo or no, this lake needs no exotic sea monster to embellish its wonder.

O'Keefe Ranch★★

Northwest of Vernon, on Hwy. 97, at the northern end of Okanagan Lake. 250-542-7868. www.okeefe ranch.ca. Open May–Sept daily 10am–5pm (Jul–Aug until 6pm). $13.50.

It's easy to see why Cornelius O'Keefe decided to stop here while driving cattle through the valley in the 1860s. The bunchgrass grew as high as a horse's belly, the breeze off the lake moderated the summer heat, and the setting still is as bucolic as ever. The ranch he built became one of the largest and most prosperous, with dozens of houses, shops, outbuildings and residents. Today this **BC Heritage Site** is the largest such historic ranch in Western Canada, with something for everyone. The **general store** is stocked with goods from the turn of the 19C. The **O'Keefe Mansion** is an elegant late-Victorian house with cut glass, wood trim and front and back stairs (the latter were for noisy children).

The annual **Cowboy Festival** in late July is a real rodeo, with cowhands from nearby ranches competing for bragging rights.

Desert Interpretive Centre★

3km/2mi north of Osoyoos on Hwy. 87. 250-495-2470 or 877-899-0897. www.desert.org. Open late Apr–mid-May and late Sept–Oct daily 10am–2pm. Late May–mid-Sept daily 9:30am–4:30pm. $7.

The southern interior of BC contains Canada's only **non-polar desert**, and this preserve, established in the late 1990s, is designed to accomplish two aims: help protect the desert, and help people understand why it's important. Take a **guided tour** along the boardwalk through the sagebrush and sand landscape; along the way, naturalists explain the hardy creatures that thrive in this challenging ecosystem, such as endangered rattlesnakes and burrowing owls.

Keremeos Grist Mill★

Upper Bench Rd., just off Hwy. 3A, in Keremeos. 43km/27mi southwest of Penticton. 250-499-2888. www.keremeos.com/gristmill. Open May–Oct daily 9am–5pm.

First opened in 1877, this restored mill occupies a pleasant, pastoral

---

U-pick Farms

For decades BC families have hopped in their cars and driven to the Okanagan to pick their own. Fruits and vegetables are available at dozens of small farms throughout the valley—from Vernon in the north to Osoyoos in the south, though most are between Penticton (an hour south of Kelowna) and Oliver, a half hour farther south, along Highway 97.

To find a U-pick farm, simply watch by the road for signs, and decide what you want. Peaches, apricots, nectarines, plums, pears, apples, strawberries, raspberries and blueberries are the major fruits; vegetables range from asparagus to zucchini, with tomatoes, corn and chilis especially popular. Prices are per pound, in the sack—the custom is that whatever you sample on-site is free. Many orchards offer picnic facilities for families who make a day trip of their fruit-picking journeys.

spot in a beautiful upland valley along the **Similkameen River**. Tall cottonwoods line the streambanks, including the small freshet that turns the grindstone (yes, it's really stone) in the gristmill. Now a **BC Heritage Site**, the mill grinds flour just as it did more than a century ago. The gift shop sells the mill's flour, ground using grains from the Prairie provinces; the flour makes great pancakes and muffins.

Kelowna★

395km/245mi east of Vancouver via Hwy. 1 East to Hwy. 5 North to Hwy. 97C South.

The biggest city in the BC interior (metro area population is about 117,000) is a small, thriving metropolis whose agricultural past is being augmented by high-tech industry and tourism. The city's resorts rely on Okanagan Lake and the valley's dependably warm summers for their existence; the burgeoning **wine industry** has become a significant draw as well. The first European settler in the area was Father Charles Pandosy, an Oblate friar who established a mission along a creek in 1860. The remarkable houses and barns he built of hand-hewn cottonwoods—artfully joined by dovetail notching—still stand at **Pandosy Mission Provincial Heritage Site★** (*Benvoulin and Casorso Rds., east Kelowna; www. okanaganhistoricalsociety.org*). The rest of Kelowna's past is on view at a complex of museums downtown, chief among which describe the viticulture and orcharding industries.

Orchard Industry Museum

1304 Ellis St. 778-478-0347. www.kelownamuseum.ca. Open year-round Tue–Fri 10am–5pm, Sat 10am–4pm, holidays 11am–3pm. Here you'll see how the industry's development depended on transportation to get the fruit to market—by boat along the lake to a railhead, then on to Vancouver. One of the museum's most delightful aspects is the collection of Art Deco-style **fruit-box labels**.

Wine Museum

1304 Ellis St. 250-868-0441. www.kelownamuseum.ca. Open year-round Mon–Fri 10am–6pm, Sat 10am–5pm, Sun and holidays 11am–5pm. Closed Jan 1, Dec 25-26. Exhibits describe how pioneers had to overcome skepticism about the industry's potential this far north; Okanagan wines are for sale in the adjacent shop.

🍷 BC Wine Country

The warm summer climate and cool nights of the **Okanagan Valley** have proven ideal for growing wine grapes, and a happy accident (that at first seemed calamitous) led to the area's signature product. When a vineyard's grapes froze on the vines one fall, the winemaker let them thaw and fermented the juice into a sweet after-dinner drink called **ice wine**—BC ice wines now enjoy huge popularity in Asia, and many grape crops are deliberately left on the vines to freeze. BC now boasts more than 200 wineries. Dozens of these operate in the valley, mostly around Kelowna and in the arid valley south of Penticton. That city's **Wine Country Visitor Centre**, similar to the one in Napa, California, has winery pamphlets, touring maps, and a shop that sells an extensive selection of Okanagan wines *(553 Vees Dr., Penticton; 250-490-2006; www.pentictonwineinfo.com; open year-round daily 9am–6pm; extended hours in summer; closed Dec 25 and Jan 1).*

Winning Wineries

• **Mission Hill Family Estate** – *1730 Mission Hill Rd., in West Kelowna. 250-768-7611. www.missionhillwinery.com. Tastings and tours daily.* Aiming to become one of the top wineries on earth (no small objective), this ambitious operation across the lake from Kelowna has invested millions of dollars in facilities—a large visitor centre, an outdoor performance amphitheatre, tasting rooms, dining rooms and extensive underground cellars. It's known for its chardonnay, merlot and ice wine.

• **Quail's Gate Estate Winery** – *3303 Boucherie Rd., Kelowna. 250-769-4451 or 800-420-9463. www.quailsgate.com. Tastings and tours daily.* Located in a 130-year-old log home, Quail's Gate winery focuses on merlot, pinot noir and chardonnay.

• **Burrowing Owl Estate Winery** – *500 Burrowing Owl Pl., Oliver. Tours daily Apr–Dec. 250-498-0620 or 877-498-0620. www.bovwine.com.* This winery is noted for its intensely flavoured reds. At the winery's **Sonora Room** restaurant, you can taste

Touring Tip

Looking for a place to stay overnight in Kelowna? The **Manteo Resort** *(3762 Lakeshore Rd.; 250-860-1031 or 800-445-5255; www.manteo.com)* offers swimming, sailing, tennis, volleyball and other recreation as well as a restaurant and guest rooms.

Tinhorn Creek winery

© Chris Mason Stearns / Tinhorn Creek

how Burrowing Owl's wines complement fine regional cuisine.

• **Tinhorn Creek** – *537 Tinhorn Creek Rod., Oliver. 250-498-3743 or 888-484-6467. www.tinhorn.com. Self-guided tours and tastings daily 10am–5pm.* Nestled against the foothills on the west side of the valley, Tinhorn is famed for varietal reds such as merlot. Nearby Tinhorn Creek was the site of a 19C gold mine.

EXCURSIONS

FOR FUN

At one end of downtown Vancouver, horse-drawn carriages trundle visitors sedately through the peaceful woods of Stanley Park. At the other end, hockey players and pucks rocket across the ice in one of the most dynamic sports of all. The opportunities for fun in Vancouver are as diverse as the city itself—and they're available year-round.

GRANVILLE ISLAND★★

On False Creek. Follow Granville St. south from downtown, then follow signs to loop back around under Granville bridge on W. 2nd Ave. Or take a ferry across False Creek (see sidebar, opposite). 604-666-6655. www.granvilleisland.com.

A busy **industrial zone** in the period between the two World Wars, then a run-down collection of warehouses, Granville Island was transformed into an effervescent district of shops, stalls, galleries and cafes in the 1970s.

Today it's a designated **heritage district** operated on behalf of the Government of Canada. It's a favourite of visitors and residents alike—especially the Public Market, where a dozen cultures mix, the variety of smells, flavours, sights and sounds is a feast for the senses, and the waterfront

views of False Creek and the Burrard Bridge are superb.

The island fills 12ha/29 acres with attractions; the place to start is the **Granville Island information kiosk** *(Johnston and Cartwright Sts.; 604-666-6655)*. Maps are available to guide you around, and the bulletin board is a colourful menu of island goings-on.

Public Market★★

Granville Island; for access, see sidebar. 604-666-6477. www.granvilleisland.com. Open year-round daily 9am–7pm. Closed Jan 1 and Dec 24–25.

A large, hangar-like building right along False Creek, the Public Market is the most-visited and best-loved facility on the island. Here you can wander among dozens of independent stalls whose offerings embrace a

---

Getting to Granville Island

Aquabus *604-689-5858; www.theaquabus.com.*
False Creek Ferries: *604-684-7781; www.granvilleislandferries.bc.ca.*

The water taxis that ply **False Creek** like little jitneys are not only colourful and quaint—they're a mighty handy way to get around the area, running from lower Granville and Burrard streets to Granville Island, Vanier Park, Science World, English Bay Bathhouse and several other locales. Rides cost $3.25–$5.50, depending on your destination; the companies' docks are easy to spot along the waterfront (if not, consult a tourist map). The schedule is simple: boats putter back and forth, dropping off passengers at their destinations, and veering into the dock when they see someone waiting for a pickup. Water taxis start running about 6:30am, and continue until 7:30pm (Aquabus) and as late as 9:30pm (False Creek Ferries).

MUST DO

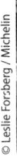

Granville Island Public Market

cosmically broad range: artisan cheese and bread, seafood, fresh BC fruits and vegetables, condiments, jams and preserves, handmade sausages, butcher-block meats, crafts, and artwork. It's impossible to leave without buying something.

Stalls that surround the two food courts serve hot food from every country imaginable, including Russian, American, Chinese, Thai, Austrian and Greek.

At **Stock Market** (*604-687-2433 www.thestockmarket.ca*), cooks brew up steaming pots of soup; ladled into a bowl with a piece of bread, this combination makes a splendid cool-season lunch. Noodles in the salads at **Zara's Pasta Deli** (*604-683-2935 www.zarasdeli.com*) are made fresh every morning, and **Kaisereck Deli** (*604-685-8810*) piles hearty meats and cheeses onto thick, dense bread. If you need a beverage to complement your lunch, **Liberty Wine Merchants**(*604-602-1120 www. libertywinemerchants.com*) boasts a large inventory of British Columbia vintages.

Must-Stop Shops

Artist studios, gift stores, and handmade craft shops surround the Public Market and are interspersed with seafood restaurants and a few nautical-themed stores that supplied the fishing boats that once populated the neighbourhood. One of the original tenants of Granville Island is local favourite **The Lobster Man** (*1807 Mast Tower; 604-687-4531*), which sells a mouth-watering variety of fresh shellfish including live crab and lobsters.

Granville Island Brewing Company

1441 Cartwright St. 604-687-2739. www.gib.ca. Daily 10am–9pm.

This brewery was the first microbrewery in Canada. Though its major production facilities, having outgrown this site, have been moved to the suburbs, small batches are still brewed here, and tours and tastings are regular events. You can vote your opinion on the experimental brews.

FOR FUN

Pirates for a Day

For a day on the water, rent a motorboat from **Sewell's Marina at Horseshoe Bay** (*6409 Bay St., West Vancouver; 604-921-3474; www.sewellsmarina.com; a 17ft 60HP for 6 people is $245 for 4hrs*). The waters of Howe Sound are usually calm, so pack a picnic lunch and let the kids pretend they are pirates while exploring the many islands and coves. The view from the water lets you see the normally hidden luxury homes along the coastline near Lions Bay, including the one used as Baltair's house in the *Battlestar Galactica* television series.

VANCOUVER LOOKOUT★

At Harbour Centre Tower, 555 W. Hastings St. 604-689-0421. www.vancouverlookout.com. Open May–Sep daily 8:30am–10:30pm. Rest of the year daily 9am–9:30pm. $15.75

Though the view from this tower-topping, circular **observation deck** is expansive—it's the highest point in Vancouver—the ride up is what many visitors remember most. The glass-enclosed elevator soars 167.5m/550ft up the outside of the building, so it's not a good choice for anyone with severe vertigo. Once you're up top, you have a 🚟 **360-degree panorama★★★** of the city, with handy signs that mark everything you see. Top of Vancouver, the restaurant atop the tower, is a unique and lofty spot in which to dine with an awesome view (*604-669-2220; www.topof vancouver.com*).

STANLEY PARK CARRIAGE TOURS

Near Stanley Park information kiosk, Stanley Park Dr. 604-681-5115. www.stanleyparktours. com. One-hour tours depart every 20min, mid-Mar–Oct daily 9:40am–5pm. $32.99 for the basic tour. For more information about Stanley Park, See Parks and Gardens.

The clip-clop of horseshoes is a much better background sound for a tour of the park than engine RPMs. This long-established company offers group tours in horse-drawn wagons, with narration to describe the sights along the way. More intimate tours in private horse-drawn carriages, known more commonly in Canada as a "caleche," are available by reservation.

JUST FOR SPORT

The city's three major-league sports franchises are quintessentially Canadian and receive heartfelt community support. Both the **Vancouver Canucks** NHL hockey team and the **BC Lions** CFL football team have made trips to their sport's championships. The Canucks qualified for the Stanley Cup finals, but lost the final game in the 2011 season to the Boston Bruins. That same year, the Lions provided some solace by winning the Grey Cup, the CFL title, the sixth time in 10 appearances when they have taken home the top prize. Why not take in a game during the season?

♦ **Vancouver Canucks** – *Rogers Arena, between the Dunsmuir and*

MUST DO

© Vancouver Lookout

Vancouver Lookout

Georgia St. viaducts. 800-745-3000. www.canucks.nhl.com. Tickets for a single game: $66–$345. Season: Oct–Jun. One of North America's most popular professional sports, **hockey** is central to Canadian life—millions of Canadians have grown up playing pick-up games on frozen lakes and rinks in community arenas. Seats sell out for most of the Canucks' home games, which can be boisterous events.

♦ **BC Lions** – *BC Place Stadium, 777 Pacific Blvd. 604-661-3626. www.bclions.com. Tickets $29-$160. Season: Jun–Oct.* Canadian **football** has three downs (as opposed to four in the States) and is played on a longer and wider field, with 12 players instead of 11. Canadians believe it is a much more exciting game than American football.

♦ **Vancouver Whitecaps** – *BC Place Stadium, 777 Pacific Blvd. 604-669-9283. www.whitecapsfc.com. Tickets $27-$71. Season: Mar–Oct.* Vancouver's Major League Soccer team has the loudest crowds of any sport in Vancouver.

♦ **Vancouver Canadians** play Single A-level minor-league baseball at charming Nat Bailey Stadium. *Jun-Sep, 604-872-5232, www.canadiansbaseball.com.*

MOWtown

With more than $1 billion of activity and more than 200 productions per year, Vancouver ranks right up there with Los Angeles, San Francisco, New York City and Toronto as a leader in North American film and video production. Because so many TV movies and series are now produced here, the city has acquired the nickname "MOWtown," for Movie of the Week.

Popular films shot in the Vancouver area include: *Carnal Knowledge* (1971); *Legends of the Fall* (1994); *X-Men* (2002); *First Blood* (1982); *Happy Gilmore* (1996); *X-2: X-Men United* (2003); *The Accused* (1988); *Double Jeopardy* (1999); *I, Robot* (2004); *Russia House* (1990); *Scooby-Doo* (2002); *X-Men: The Last Stand* (2006); *Twilight New Moon* (2010); *Mission Impossible 4* (2011); and *Twilight Breaking Dawn* (2011).

FOR FUN

OUTDOOR FUN

Snowcapped mountains, glistening blue water and serene forests beckon everywhere you look in and around Vancouver, so it's no surprise that opportunities for outdoor recreation are practically infinite. The list includes sailing, swimming, skating, biking, in-line skating, skiing, snowshoeing, kayaking and canoeing. The city is known as a place where you can ski, sail and golf all in the same day, and energetic souls have done exactly that. A more mellow (and rational) approach is to spread the adventures out a bit. By skiing one day, kayaking the next, 🚲 biking around Stanley Park after that—there's no chance you'll run out of things to do.

🚢 HARBOUR CRUISES★

1 N. Denman St., in Coal Harbour. 604-688-7246 or 800-663-1500. www.boatcruises.com. $30–$70; $80 for dinner cruises. Call for schedule.

Spectacular as Vancouver is from almost any angle, the most sensational way to see the cityscape is from the water that encircles it. Harbour cruises are hour-long narrated tours of the harbour; luncheon cruises head up **Indian Arm**, the mountain-ringed fjord just northeast of Burrard Inlet; and sunset dinner cruises run from Burrard Inlet over to **English Bay**, and out into the **Georgia Strait** and back. Sunset Dinner cruises *(2.5hrs)* offer live music, plus a West-Coast themed menu. You won't soon forget the sight of Vancouver's skyscrapers backlit by the sun dropping over **Vancouver Island**; the perspective gained by being on the water adds greatly to your understanding of what is, after all, a maritime world capital.

IN THE SWIM

Yes, Vancouver has swimming weather—three good months of it, from early July to mid-September—and the city's two

major **outdoor pools** draw throngs on sunny days.

◆ **Pool at Second Beach** – *Stanley Park Dr. 604-257-8371. $5.76.* Located in the southwest part of Stanley Park, Second Beach pool once held unheated salt water. Now filled with heated fresh water and outfitted with slides for kids, the pool still enjoys fresh breezes off English Bay.

◆ **Kitsilano Pool** – *2305 Cornwall Ave. 604-731-0011. $5.76.* Directly across the bay, at the intersection of Arbutus and Cornwall streets, the famed Kitsilano pool is the largest **saltwater pool** in Canada—and it's even heated.

🏖 JUST BEACHY

Vancouver's 12.5km/11mi of **beaches** not only are scenic, they offer a distinct variety of things to do. Sorry, no dogs (there are dog-friendly sections) or alcohol allowed. Other restrictions include: no smoking, no kites, no ball-playing except in designated areas, no fires (BBQ pits are acceptable), and no inflatable water toys. Lifeguards are on duty Victoria Day to Labour Day daily 11:30am–9pm. For information, call 3-1-1, or from outside Vancouver, 604-873-7000. (*mid-May–mid-Sept; www.*

Harbour Cruises, sunset cruise

vancouver.ca/parks-recreation-culture/beaches).

◆ **English Bay Beach★★** – *Beach Ave. at Denman St.* A great place to swim, kayak, picnic and **people-watch**.

◆ **Third Beach★** – *West side of Stanley Park.* One of Stanley Park's two beaches, Third Beach is popular with locals who come to swim and sunbathe.

◆ **Jericho Beach** – *West end of Point Grey Rd.* Go fly a kite, enjoy a sunset or fish off the pier here.

◆ **Kitsilano Beach** – *North end of Yew St. at the waterfront.* Kitsilano's neighbourhood beach and volleyball courts are magnets for sun worshippers.

◆ **Wreck Beach** – If you're interested in an all-over tan, this beach is one of Canada's most popular **nude beaches** *(steps lead to beach near the intersection of N.W. Marine Dr. and University Blvd., west of UBC campus).*

Kayaking English Bay

Ecomarine Ocean Kayak Centre is located at 1668 Duranleau St. 604-689-7575 or 1-888-425-2925. www.ecomarine.com. Early Jun–Labour Day daily 10:30am–1pm and 2pm–4:30pm. $39 for 2hrs for single kayaks; $49 for 2hrs for double kayaks.

Sea lions and harbour seals pop their heads above water to inspect you. Lovers stroll by on the Stanley Park seawall, oblivious to your presence. The salt tang of the air clears your head, and the insistent tug of the tide competes with the gentle roll of the swells to pull you this way and that.

Ocean kayaking is a sensory pleasure anywhere—in Vancouver, following the south Stanley Park shoreline, it's a wholly unexpected urban adventure.

Ecomarine rents single and double kayaks ; if you don't venture out into the sea lanes, little experience is needed. **Third Beach** is the best destination, where you can haul out on the warm sand for a picnic lunch before you head back in.

GO FISH

If you thought that **salmon fishing** was rare, you haven't heard the whole story. True, some species of salmon are threatened—but others are thriving. In an average year, the **Fraser River** draws up

OUTDOOR FUN

Pacific Salmon

Born in freshwater streams and rivers, sometimes hundreds of miles from the sea, salmon migrate to the sea to mature. After two or more years growing in the ocean, they return to the stream of their birth to spawn and (usually) die. There are **five types** of Pacific salmon—chinook (king), coho (silver), sockeye (red), pink (humpy) and chum. **Steelhead** is a type of trout that also migrates to sea and returns to fresh water to spawn, sometimes more than once. Some salmon reach magnificent size, more than 22.6kg/50 pounds. Unfortunately, several species in lower BC and in the US face survival challenges, chiefly from overfishing, logging, and habitat destruction.

The Vancouver Aquarium (see For Kids) in Stanley Park has created a salmon **spawning stream**, which runs a mere 91m/300ft from Coal Harbour up to the grounds of the aquarium. Fish first stocked here in the late 1990s have established active runs that return to spawn each October.

to 7 million salmon returning to spawn. Federal fisheries managers monitor salmon stocks closely to set seasons and catch limits, and many opportunities remain for visitors to go salmon fishing. Many **charter operators** these days encourage their clients to practice **catch-and-release**, but you can also have your fish frozen and shipped home. Seasons vary among species, but summertime is the peak season.

Most of Vancouver's charter fleet operates out of the marina at **Granville Island**. Rates vary widely (*$75–$550/person*), depending on the duration of the trip, number of people and distance travelled.

♦ In Vancouver, **Bites-on Salmon Charters** (*877-688-2483; www. bites-on.com*) offers trips that leave from downtown.

The Lower Mainland still has an active commercial fishery, too. Wander by the **False Creek Fishermen's Wharf** (*east end of W. 1st Ave., just west of Granville Island*) to see (and buy) the fresh catch of the day, which might range from crab and shrimp to salmon and octopus.

WATCHING WILDLIFE

The huge wilderness that surrounds Vancouver holds a healthy array of wild creatures, ranging from **tidepool anemones** to gargantuan whales. Almost all have been subjected to consumptive use in the past, but legal and social changes are shifting the most popular wildlife activity from harvesting it to watching it. BC has more than 450 species of birds (many are migratory), from the **Canada goose** and **Great Blue Heron** to ravens and gray jays.

You can see many wild animals—from squirrels to **harbour seals**—simply by strolling through 🐾 **Stanley Park**, but the more exotic species are the subjects of guided trips that delight thousands of visitors every year. In BC, whale-, eagle- and bear-watching lead the list. The first two are accessible from Vancouver; bear-watching tours require overnight travel from Vancouver (*contact Tourism BC; see Practical Information*).

♦ 🐾 **Whales** – Despite the fact that over the centuries whalers

Humpback whale

© John.Carnemolla/istockphoto.com

nearly harpooned them to extinction, more than 20,000 **gray whales** still ply the migration route between the Bering Sea and Mexico each spring and winter. Gray and **humpback whales** and **orcas** (the latter also known as killer whales)—several pods (family groups) of which inhabit Georgia Strait and Puget Sound—can be seen on day trips that depart from Vancouver. Most charter operators depart from Victoria (*see Excursions*), but **Vancouver Whale Watch** *(604-274-9565; www.vancouverwhalewatch.com)* runs shuttles from downtown Vancouver to its dock in Richmond. Daily departures *(Apr–Oct)* utilize Zodiac-type vessels, and on all trips naturalists are onboard.

♦ **Bald Eagles** – One of the largest concentrations of bald eagles in North America returns every winter to the **Squamish River**, an hour north of Vancouver, to feed on a rare winter salmon run. As many as 3,700 eagles roost in the cottonwoods along the river. **Canadian Outback Adventures & Events** leads two-hour **raft** float trips down the river to view the eagles. The mountain-rimmed valley makes a beautiful setting in which to see the birds *(late Nov–Feb Thu–Sun, departing 10am; 800-565-8735; www.canadianoutback.com; $100 fee includes transportation from downtown and Whistler hotels, a light lunch with hot chocolate and use of suitable clothing)*.

Fast Facts about Whales

- Like all mammals, whales are warm-blooded: they breathe air, and maintain a constant body temperature.
- **Gray whales** (*Eschrichtius robustus*) make the longest seasonal migration of any whales, travelling about 20,000km/12,500mi each year.
- **Orcas** (*Orcinus orca*), or killer whales, are actually a type of dolphin.
- Bigger than any dinosaur, the **blue whale** (*Balaenoptera musculus*) is the largest animal ever to inhabit the earth. A blue whale can grow up to 34m/110ft long and weigh as much as 180,000kg/174 tons.

OUTDOOR FUN

113

FOR KIDS

Sandy beaches, majestic forests, snowy mountains and hundreds of small parks and play areas—not to mention a world-class aquarium and several interactive museums—make Vancouver a remarkably kid-friendly place. Though the formal attractions for children are excellent, don't forget that a short walk along the shoreline seawall to look for seals and crabs will delight your little ones as well.

Stanley Park★★★ for Kids

Northwest end of downtown.
See Parks and Gardens.

Stanley Park is the undisputed capital for young fun in Vancouver. The park's pleasures can be as simple as stopping to watch squirrels play, or building sand castles at one of its **three beaches**. Star of Stanley Park, the Vancouver Aquarium is a facility that will entertain the entire family.

🐟 Vancouver Aquarium★★★

Southeast corner of Stanley Park, at Avison Way. 604-659-3474. www.vanaqua.org. Open daily 10:00am–5pm, 9:30–6pm in summer and on holiday weekends. $29, children $15.

A day here is not just fun—it's good for the world we live in, as the Vancouver Aquarium has become one of the leading conservation enterprises in North America. Some of the beautiful and exotic sea creatures it introduces to thousands of awe-struck humans are threatened in some way, and the aquarium works hard to help them survive and to help visitors understand what that entails.

In 2014 the aquarium unveiled the first phase of an extensive ongoing renovation that nearly doubled its gallery space, and added digital screens, a new entry complex, and a 140-seat theatre.

All the traditional favourites are still here too: superbly athletic marine mammals entertain the hundreds of delighted spectators who ring the arena pool. **Sea otters** frolic with balls in their enclosures. Trainers step into tropical exhibits to toss food to the **crocodiles** (one of the most popular daily events here). But throughout, the emphasis is on explaining the habitat needs, daily lives and ecological significance of the animals to encourage support for conservation.

The aquarium's famed orcas are gone, having died of old age

Just for Kids

Ever wanted to spend the night with a shark? You can, in a manner of speaking, during the Vancouver Aquarium's **sleepovers**, when kids get to spend the night in sleeping bags among the galleries. Or have a "beluga encounter" and go behind the scenes to feed these charming creatures, experience their unique communication style, and even pat their tongues. At **Clownfish Cove** play area, tots can dress up as their favourite sea creature.

or been sent to other marine parks, and daily shows now draw audiences with **beluga whales**—an exotic species for which the aquarium is one of the world's leading advocacy and research institutions. And while the shows are hugely entertaining, the "acts" are drawn from beluga real life: when one of the whales pokes its head above the surface to spout water all over a trainer (kids take great delight in this), it represents a behaviour belugas use to dislodge food from the floor of their home waters in the Arctic.

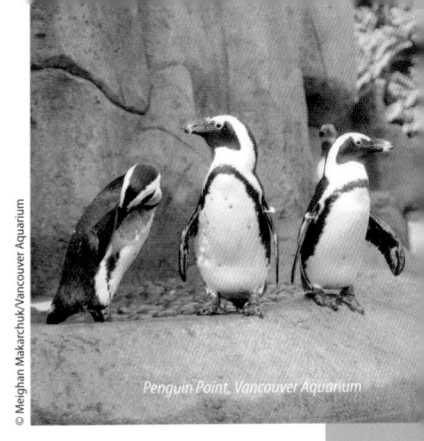
© Meighan Makarchuk/Vancouver Aquarium

Penguin Point, Vancouver Aquarium

Encounters with Fish and Other Creatures

Check schedules for feedings and show times when you buy your ticket.

◆ **Graham Amazon Gallery** — This indoor wing has caymans, crocodiles, anacondas, **piranhas** and the world's largest freshwater fish, a type of **gar** that grows to 3.6m/12ft in length. Don't miss the daily crocodile feedings.

◆ **Pacific Canada** — This large pavilion depicts the rich and colourful marine environment along the British Columbia coast, down to the surging tides that wash and nurture orange sunflower **starfish**, chartreuse **sea anemones**, and delicate cream-coloured **nudibranchs**.

◆ **Canada's Arctic** — Exploring the vast, dramatic water wilderness that is home to belugas and their northern aquatic neighbours, this exhibit showcases the extreme changes endured by marine life in the remote Far North.

◆ **Penguin Point** — Enjoy learning about these dapperly dressed, diverse birds as they walk and swim about their special space, a replica of their natural **South African** habitat; it's possible to get fairly up-close and friendly with these remarkable birds.

🚂 Miniature Railway and Children's Farmyard

West of Vancouver Aquarium. 604-257-8531. www.city. vancouver.bc.ca/parks/parks/ stanley. Open Jun–Sept Mon–Thu 11am–4pm; Fri–Sun and holidays 11am–5pm. $6.

In 1886, Canadian Pacific locomotive No. 374 pulled into the Vancouver rail yards, completing the first train transit of Canada. The engine pulling the Stanley Park miniature train is an exact replica of Engine 374, a fact that means more to the adults than to the kids they accompany on the train. Children just enjoy the 15-minute ride through the towering cedars and firs along a small rise in the park.

In the adjacent 🚂 **farmyard**, kids can pet the tamer animals among the sheep, goats, pigs, cows, chickens, ducks—and one llama.

The **Vancouver Trolley Company** *(604-801-5515 or 888-451-5581; www.vancouvertrolley.com)* offers tours and "hop-on, hop-off" city explorations year-round, including a Stanley Park Shuttle service. Trips on the red-painted cable cars can be day-long or point-to-point. Family **Goose Tours** are popular. The trolleys also operate in and around Victoria. *Sample 1-day fare $40; Stanley Park Shuttle $10.*

BC Sports Hall of Fame★

777 Pacific Blvd., in BC Place Stadium. 604-687-5520. www.bcsportshalloffame.com. Open daily 10am–5pm. $15, children over 5 years $12.

Sports in BC go way back to the **war-canoe races** First Nations residents held two centuries ago. Packed exhibit galleries in this comprehensive museum trace the **snowshoe races** prospectors held for entertainment to the 1998 Olympics victory by Whistler resident Ross Rebagliati, who won the first **snowboard** gold medal ever. Kids wandering these halls peer up at sports legends past and present, from **curling** to **lacrosse**.

Check out the **Hall of Champions** or the **Aboriginal Sport Gallery** that pays homage to the sports culture of BC First Nations peoples. New to the complex is a tribute to the Vancouver 2010 Olympics, including the opening ceremonies, awarding of medals and a replica of Roberto Luongo's goalie mask.

H.R. MacMillan Space Centre★

1100 Chestnut St., in Vanier Park. 604-738-7827. www.spacecentre.ca. Open year-round Sat and holidays 10am–5pm, Sun noon–5pm, Mon–Fri 10am–3pm; Sat astronomy 7:30pm–9pm; observatory opens 8pm. Closed Dec 25. $18, children $15 (eve $13); observatory by donation.

Located next to the Vancouver Museum, this facility crams a lot into a small space. Exhibits explain the basics of planetary orbits, the nature of galaxies and the history of human space exploration.

A special section delineates Canadian contributions to the latter. Highlights are a **motion simulator**, which takes a virtual trip to Mars, the moon, and other extraterrestrial locales; and a compact **planetarium** in which **laser light shows** are wedded to

Granville Island Children's Market

Granville Island. Follow Granville St. south from downtown, then follow signs to loop back around under Granville bridge on W. 2nd Ave. Access also via ferry (see For Fun). 604-689-8477. www.kidsmarket.ca. Open year-round daily 10am–6pm. "Daddy, may I have that?" Be prepared to hear that plea dozens of times at this aggregation of stores at the entrance to Granville Island. The multicoloured building holds 30 shops selling everything from model trains to games to dolls, in greater quantity and variety than you're likely to find anywhere else in town. The shops emphasize items handmade by local artisans.

Vancouver International Children's Festival

Granville Island, late May. 604-708-5655. www.childrensfestival.ca.

This old-fashioned fair delights kids as much today as it did when it began more than three decades ago. In 2011 the festival moved from Vanier Park to Granville Island, but the setup is similar: tents and playgrounds are erected for the Monday to Sunday affair, designed to entertain entire families. Mimes, jugglers, clowns and singers stroll the grounds; **puppet shows** and plays take place on various stages. Cotton candy, hot dogs, lemonade, a **petting zoo**, stilt-walkers, sack races—there's something for everyone. *Entrance fee $8; shows package $25.*

rock music by the eternally popular Pink Floyd, or Canadian stars such as Avril Lavigne.

Maplewood Farm

405 Seymour River Pl., North Vancouver. 604-929-5610. www.maplewoodfarm.bc.ca. Open May–mid-Sept daily 10am–4pm. Rest of year Tue–Sun 10am–4pm. Closed Dec 25. $7.55, children $4.55.

Why do pigs wallow in the mud, and goats butt heads? You'll learn the answer to these questions and more at this once-thriving dairy farm, the last surviving agricultural enterprise on the North Shore when the regional Parks Board took it over to save it from development. Maplewood occupies a pastoral, tree-shaded spot along a creek, and it's hard to tell who's happier within its bounds—the 200 domestic animals and birds that live there, or the hundreds of kids who visit on sunny days. The ponies, goats, sheep, cows, ducks, geese and squealing pigs here are all well used to the intense attention children pay them.

Touring Tip

The fun way to get to Science World is on the **Aquabus**, the colourful little tubs that ply False Creek (*see For Fun*).

Science World BC

1455 Quebec St. 604-443-7440. www.scienceworld.ca. Open Jun–Sept daily 10am–6pm. Rest of the year Tue–Fri 10am–4pm, Sat, Sun and holidays 10am–6pm. $22.50, children $15.25 . Separate fee for the Omnimax theatre.

This spherical **geodesic dome** perched at the end of False Creek may be the last structure remaining from Expo '86. Today what is affectionately known as the "golf ball" houses an **Omnimax theatre** as well as an astounding number of **interactive exhibits** and games that appeal to both adults and children. Geology, physics, electronics, biology, marine studies, zoology, physiology— hardly any scientific discipline is overlooked. For starters, visitors use synthesizers to make music; create square bubbles; generate plasma and electrical charges; and watch waves sweep the ocean floor.

FOR KIDS

117

PERFORMING ARTS

Sure, Vancouver is a centre for the film and broadcast industry, but it's also a breeding ground for Canadian music. Stars who have begun or developed their careers here include actor Michael J. Fox, singers Diana Krall, Bryan Adams, Michael Bublé (born in Burnaby) and Sarah McLachlan, and famed classical pianist Jon Kimura Parker. Symphony, opera, drama and dance alone will provide culture vultures with plenty of performances to keep them clapping in Vancouver.

Orpheum Theatre★
601 Smithe St. 604-665-3035. www.vancouver.ca/parks-recreation-culture/the-orpheum.aspx.
Designated a National Historic Site in 1979, the Orpheum is a one-of-a-kind arts palace from the era when the sky was the limit for theatre design.
Opened in 1927, the 2,800-seat hall was once the largest theatre in Canada. Interior arches, columns and moldings of travertine, marble, stone and plaster were designed in Spanish Baroque style by Scottish architect Marcus Priteca. Converted to a movie theatre, it was scheduled to be divided up until community pressure in the mid-1970s spurred the city to buy the building and renovate it for use by the symphony.
Today the theatre is once again a glittering performance venue with few equals, hosting contemporary and classical musical performances that range from Steve Winwood to Jesse Cook. The original 🐜 **pipe organ** still plays in half a dozen symphony concerts each year.

Arts Club Theatre
Granville Island, 1585 Johnston St. 604-687-1644. www.artsclub.com.
This busy and successful nonprofit theatre company is the one from which Michael J. Fox embarked on his TV and film career. It now mounts productions on three stages—two on Granville Island and one at the **Stanley Stage** (*see p 119*). The company's offerings range from avant-garde drama to classic musical comedy, with occasional original productions.

Centre in Vancouver for Performing Arts
777 Homer St. 604-602-0616. www.livevan.com/centrein vancouver_com.

Tickets Tonight

Tickets for many musical and theatrical performances can be had for half price on the day of the show at **Tickets Tonight**, in the main Tourism Vancouver Visitor Centre (*Plaza Level, 200 Burrard St.; 604-684-2787; www.ticketstonight.ca*).

The **Alliance for Arts & Culture** is a clearinghouse for 350 performance arts of all kinds in Vancouver; it maintains a comprehensive schedule of events at its office at 938 Howe Street (*604-681-3535; www.allianceforarts.com*).

MUST DO

© The Vancouver Symphony Orchestra

Orpheum Theatre

Once known as the Ford Centre, this striking building across from Library Square was designed by renowned architect **Moshe Safdie**. The conical glass tower over the entrance is one of those love-it-or-hate-it designs that modern architecture seems to relish. Known for its superb acoustics, the centre is Vancouver's venue for touring pop stars and visiting **Broadway musicals**.

🎭 Queen Elizabeth Theatre
649 Cambie St., Hamilton and Dunsmuir Sts. 604-665-3050. www. vancouver.ca/parks-recreation-culture/queen-elizabeth-theatre.
Home to the city's opera company as well as its principal ballet troupe, this 2,800-seat theatre boasts a 70ft-wide proscenium arch stage. The **Vancouver Opera Company** (*604-683-0222; www. vancouveropera.ca*) offers four or five productions a year here, ranging from standard—Mozart, Puccini, Verdi—to original

productions that tend toward the avant-garde. People still talk about a notorious production of Strauss' *Salome*, in the mid-1990s, that was directed by Canadian filmmaker Atom Egoyan. **Ballet British Columbia** also struts its stuff at the "Queen-E," as it's called (*604-732-5003; www.balletbc.com*).

Stanley Industrial Alliance Stage
2750 Granville St. 604-687-1644. www.artsclub.com.
A massive community fund-raising project enabled the Arts Club Theatre company to take over this historic Art Deco building in 1998. Restored to their 1930s grandeur, the theatre's friezes, sconces and chandeliers glisten anew. Productions here tend to be revues, musicals and classic Broadway plays.

Vancouver Symphony
833 Seymour St. 604-876-3434 or 604-684-9100. www.vancouver symphony.ca.

PERFORMING ARTS

While it regularly presents classic works by Beethoven, Brahms, Tchaikovsky and Mahler, the Vancouver Symphony frequently performs and occasionally commissions works by **Western Canada** composers during its year-long season; these pieces often incorporate elements of First Nations music. Local musicians are featured, too, including members of the prodigious Parker clan, whose three sons are all established pianists. The symphony shares the Orpheum Theatre *(see p 118)* with other local and national touring companies.

More Musts for Performing Arts

Chan Centre for the Performing Arts – *6265 Crescent Rd., University of British Columbia campus. 604-822-9197. www.chancentre.com.* This sparkling facility at UBC is an elegant mid-size performance hall that welcomes national stars to its three stages.

Dal Richards Orchestra – *604-681-6060. www.dalrichards.com.* Western Canada's leading practitioners of big band and swing music make regular appearances throughout the Lower Mainland. Richards has been feature entertainer on special Holland America Lines' Alaska cruises, departing from Vancouver.

The Dance Centre – *604-606-6400. www.thedancecentre.ca.* Vancouver is a hotbed for modern and 🏮 **ethnic dance**— especially Chinese, Japanese and Indian—and this clearinghouse organization maintains a schedule of performances at various venues.

Firehall Arts Centre – *280 E. Cordova St. 604-689-0926.*

www.firehallartscentre.ca. Firehall hosts avant-garde drama and performance art, both local and touring, on the east side of downtown.

Vancouver East Cultural Centre – *1895 Venables St. 604-251-1363. www.vecc.bc.ca.* Live music and theatre hold the stage at this unusual historic venue, the renovated 1909 Grandview Methodist Church.

Vancouver TheatreSports League – *1502 Duranleau St., Granville Island. 604-738-7013. www.vtsl.com.* This legendary troupe focuses on impromptu comedy and audience-participation events—giving an astounding 260 performances a year at the Improv Centre.

Festive Indeed

If you like festivals, you've come to the right place. Vancouver shows its dedication to the arts through a stellar, year-long lineup of festivals devoted to performance and cultural arts. Check the alternative weekly newspaper *Georgia Straight (www.straight.com)* or visit www.vancouverfestivals.info to see what's happening when you're in town.

Celebration of Light

English Bay. www.honda celebrationoflight.com. What's unique about Vancouver's annual two- to four-night showcase *(late Jul–early Aug)* is that the fireworks shower over English Bay to intensify the visual experience. The display is keyed to music, and fireworks artists from three countries compete against each other for first prize. It's free, too; the best seats are

Starry, Starry Nights

Two outdoor venues offer theatre performances under the summer skies in Vancouver, both in city parks:

• 🎭 **Theatre Under the Stars** takes place in Stanley Park's Malkin Bowl, a 1,200-seat amphitheatre set in a fir and cedar forest near the Vancouver Aquarium. Performances of repertory plays, usually musicals, take place from mid-July through August *(604-734-1917; www.tuts.ca)*.

• 🎭 **Bard on the Beach** is a summer-long Shakespeare festival staged in Vanier Park, near the start of False Creek *(take Burrard St. Bridge south and turn right on Chestnut St.)*. Elizabethan-style tents, and musical and juggling acts contribute to the festival atmosphere. The city skyline and North Shore Mountains provide the backdrop for the open stage. Three or four Shakespeare plays rotate during the seasonal schedule *(Jun–Sept; 604-739-0559 or 877-739-0559; www.bardonthebeach.org)*.

along English Bay Beach (the very best seats are at the reserved-seating barbecue at English Bay Bathhouse), but the show is visible from Kitsilano and the lower end of False Creek as well. If you want to be up close, arrive in late afternoon—thousands of people jockey for position.

🎵 Vancouver Folk Music Festival

Jericho Beach. 604-602-9798. www.thefestival.bc.ca. Folk artists from around North America perform dozens of different musical styles, from Tejano to French-Canadian, at Jericho Beach, in mid-July.

Vancouver Fringe Festival

Various locations. 604-257-0350. www.vancouverfringe.com. Fringe is perfect for a city whose political and cultural climate is Canada's most progressive. At this two-week festival in mid-September, you'll see performance art, impromptu groups, radical drama and multimedia presentations.

Vancouver International Film Festival

Various locations. 604-683-3456. www.viff.org. The stars come out between late September and mid-October for this annual affair. Though it focuses somewhat on Canadian cinema, 300 films from 50 countries are included.

🎵 Vancouver International Jazz Festival

Various locations. 604-872-5200. www.coastaljazz.ca. This annual two-week affair at the end of June draws stars from around the world. More than a dozen venues participate, from intimate nightclubs to mid-size performance halls. Don't miss the two-day street festival in Gastown and Yaletown.

SHOPPING

Vancouver's remarkable cultural diversity—with its European, Asian and Native heritages—makes shopping here a treat. Here you'll find items not available in most other North American cities, including traditional First Nations mask art and nontraditional chocolate truffles shaped to look like First Nations art. Asian foodstuffs and furnishings in Chinatown complement European antiques along Main Street, while American visitors visit the city's tobacconists for Cuban cigars, forbidden in the States.

Robson Street★★

Once known as "Robsonstrasse" to reflect the street's erstwhile German character, this thoroughfare leading from downtown to the West End has transformed itself into a cosmopolitan district with ethnic flair. It is particularly popular with Asian teens, whose main objective for flying across the Pacific is, apparently, to stroll Robson. On the blocks of Robson between Hornby and Denman streets, you can wear out your wallet buying everything from high fashion to yoga togs. When you're ready for a break, Robson is a prime place to 🚶 people-watch. Grab a seat at an outdoor cafe and check out the leather-clad bikers sipping lattés at Starbucks; purple-haired counterculture advocates heading for a demonstration at the

Vancouver Art Gallery; Japanese schoolgirls walking hand-in-hand from boutique to boutique; and smartly clad office workers scurrying back from lunch. It's a parade you won't soon forget.

Robson Street Sampler

♦ **Lush** (no. 1020; 604-687-5874; www.lush.ca) is a British soap and cosmetics maker whose delectable aromas drift out onto the street.

♦ **La Vie en Rose** (no. 1009; 604-684-5600; www.lavieenrose.ca) purveys fine European lingerie.

♦ **Roots Canada** (no. 1001; 604-683-4305; www.roots.com) is a branch of the clothing company that achieved world renown with its popularity at the Salt Lake Winter Olympics in 2002.

Great Gear for the Great Outdoors

The east end of the Broadway district is fast becoming a mecca for all manner of outdoor and recreational supplies. **Mountain Equipment Co-op** (130 W. Broadway; 604-872-7858; www.mec.ca), a home-grown Vancouver institution that resembles its American counterpart REI, carries high-quality sporting gear of every description. Store personnel here also have a priceless inventory of information; ask them if you want to know something about outdoor recreation in Western Canada. On the other side of the street, **Altus Mountain Gear** has whatever you need for a Coast Mountains-climbing expedition (137 W. Broadway; 604-876-5255).

MUST DO

Lonsdale Quay

Antiques Row
South Main St., between 16th and 25th Ave.
The usual selection of furniture, crockery and jewellery is here, with a tilt toward British Colonial leftovers, and a new emphasis on Retro and Vintage from the 1950s and 60s. **Second Time Around**, which carries both eras and a lot in between, is located at 4428 Main Street and has twice been voted the number one antiques shop in Vancouver *(604-879-2313, www.sta-antiques.com)*.

The Hudson's Bay
674 Granville St. 604-681-6211. www.thebay.com.
Yes, this retailer is the corporate descendant of the Hudson's Bay Company, whose traders established most of the first European outposts in Canada. Housed in a massive Beaux-Arts building downtown, the Bay has morphed into a mainstream department store. But you can still get **Hudson's Bay blankets**, just as trappers and traders did 150 years ago—you'd have trouble bartering for them with beaver skins, though.

Lonsdale Quay
On the North Shore of Burrard Inlet. 604-985-6261. www.lonsdale quay.com. Open year-round daily 9:30am–6:30pm (Fri until 9pm; restaurants open later).
Aside from the array of farm-fresh produce and 90 shops and cafes that await shoppers here, the best part about Lonsdale Quay is getting there. Take the **Seabus** ferry, which docks right at the quay and provides dandy views of the North Shore Mountains and downtown Vancouver en route.

Sinclair Centre
757 W. Hastings St., at Granville St. 604-488-0672. www.sinclair centre.com. See Landmarks.
Four historic buildings downtown are now linked under one glass roof as an attractive retail complex featuring **designer boutiques**, along with federal government offices.

Shopping Districts
♦ **Chinatown★** – *Bounded by Keefer, Abbott, Hastings and Gore Sts. See Neighbourhoods.*
♦ **Gastown★** – *Water St. between Carrall and Richard Sts. See Historic*

SHOPPING

123

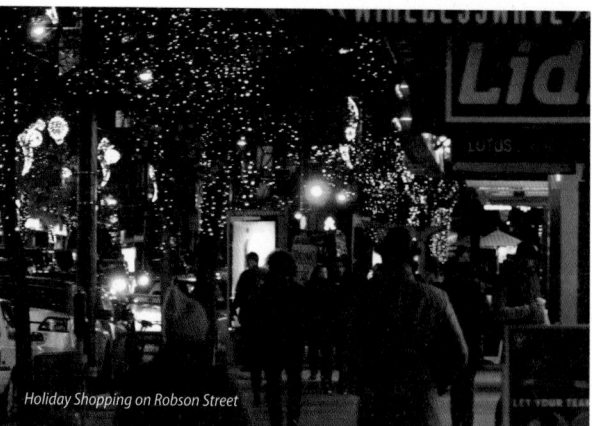

Holiday Shopping on Robson Street

© Collin Morrison / Michelin

Sites. Gastown is home to an array of T-shirt and 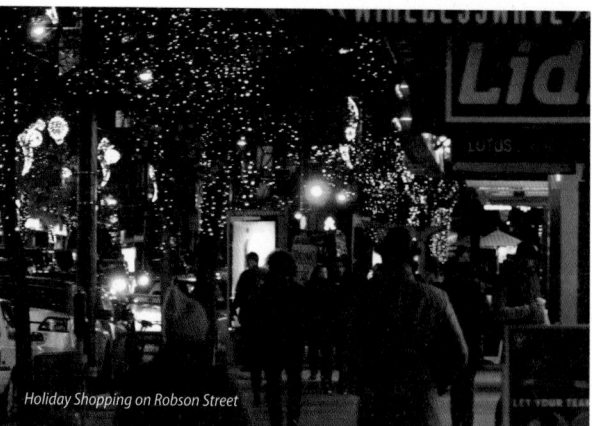 **souvenir** shops, chiefly along Water Street (need a little can of maple syrup from Quebec?), while the adjoining streets have more interesting retail outlets, like Westernwear stores, curio shops, home furnishings, and inexpensive Native artwork.

Gastown Standouts

For anyone who likes classical and world music—that's all that's sold here—**Sikora's Classical Records** *(432 West Hastings St.; 604-685-0625 or 866-685-0625; www.sikorasclassical.com)* is a treasure trove, with more than 10,000 titles. At **McLeod's Books** *(455 W. Pender St; 604-681-7654)* tables and shelves are piled high with used volumes spanning an array of subjects and authors far beyond the ken of modern chain outlets. Look here for the best in antiquarian books, many of those about Canadian history.

♦ **Yaletown★** – *Bounded by Davie, Homer, Nelson and Cambie Sts., and Pacific Blvd. See Neighbourhoods.*

♦ **Broadway District** – *Broadway and 4th Ave., roughly from Oak St. west to Arbutus St.* Vancouver's most extensive retail area is a mile-long stretch of Broadway and 4th Avenue, south of False Creek. The district is chockablock with stores, cafes and galleries, virtually all of which are independent; many concentrate on locally made or Canadian goods. Some of the beautifully shaped confections at **Chocolate Arts** *(1620 W. 3rd Ave.; 604-739-0475 or 877-739-0475; www.chocolate arts.com)* bear First Nations designs—eagles, orcas, ravens—but they pose an existential dilemma: eating the chocolate destroys the art. Check out the seasonal line; in autumn, for example, you can purchase scrumptious pumpkin pralines.

♦ **Denman Street** – *West End. See Neighbourhoods.*

MUST DO

First Nations Art

Masks, carvings, wood panels and bentwood boxes made by Western Canada's First Nations artisans are among the world's most distinctive artworks, instantly recognizable and immensely valuable. Any collector would treasure a cedar panel with vividly etched and brightly coloured illustrations of the whales, bears, eagles and ravens that are significant spirits to British Columbia's coastal peoples. Especially hard to find (and hard to make) are bentwood boxes, in which the cedar panels are formed into four sides, usually adorned with discreet decorative designs. Be aware that not all is made by First Nations people (non-authentic stores have been known to show "made in China" labels); and not all is even very good. If you care about the authenticity of a piece, your best course is to buy at a top-quality, reputable dealer—and expect to pay top dollar. Of course, what you get is the equal, in aesthetic and financial value, of any fine European or American painting. The best Inuit soapstone sculptures and Northwest Coast masks and wall panels can cost many thousands of dollars.

Best Outlets for First Nations Art

◆ **Marion Scott Gallery** (2423 Granville St., Gastown; 604-685-1934; www.marionscottgallery.com) has an especially fine selection of Inuit stone and ivory carvings, as well as prints.

◆ **Spirit Wrestler Gallery** (47 Water St.; Gastown; 604-669-8813 or 888-669-8813; www.spiritwrestler.com) specializes

Must Not Take Home

One of the great attractions of Vancouver shopping—for some Americans, at least—is that Cuban rum and cigars are freely available. US customs officials at Vancouver airports and the border are ever on the watch for these items. But it's perfectly legal to puff on a Cohiba cigar or imbibe Havana Club rum while in Canada. Just make sure you dispose of contents, bottles and wrappers before you leave the country.

in Inuit carving and Northwest Coast masks, and also carries New Zealand Maori pieces.

◆ **Hill's Native Art** (165 Water St., Gastown; 604-685-4249 or 866-685-5422; www.hillsnativeart.com) is the most reputable dealer for less expensive First Nations art, and stocks boxes, masks, totems and other carvings. There are branch stores in Victoria, Nanaimo and Duncan.

◆ **Eagle Spirit Gallery** (1803 Maritime Mews, Granville Island; 604-801-5277 or 888-801-5277; www.eaglespiritgallery.com) features superlative Northwest Coast masks and totems, all splendidly displayed.

Richmond

◆ **International Travel Maps** (12300 Bridgeport Rd. 604-273-1400) does a mostly online business, but the company has a large warehouse-style store in Richmond. A huge selection of travel books and maps makes it a popular place to shop.

NIGHTLIFE

Though Vancouver is a film- and music-industry capital, raves and disco don't cut it here. Search out the city's nightlife in the low-key lounges of its major hotels, in the many small restaurant/nightclubs that feature live music, or, if your tastes tend that way, in the huge, heaving, cocktail-fueled dance palaces in Gastown and on Granville St. For updates, see a free copy of the alternative weekly, *Georgia Straight*, or the Thursday entertainment section of the *Vancouver Sun*.

Bacchus Lounge

845 Hornby St., in the Wedgewood Hotel, Downtown. 604-608-5319. www.wedgewoodhotel.com/ hotel/bacchus.

When you see the languorous painting of Bacchus that hangs over the piano in this elegant restaurant and nightspot, you'll know its prevailing philosophy: indulge yourself, peacefully. Jazz musicians ply the keyboards here most nights of the week.

Bar None

1222 Hamilton St., Yaletown. 604-689-7000. www.barnone nightclub.ca

With almost a homey feel, thanks to its natural brick walls, wood accents and cosy leather banquettes, Bar None attracts countless celebrities to its New York-style ambience. Live bands play here, but most of the Top 40, dance, house and hip-hop is spun by resident or guest DJs.

Brooklyn

91 Powell St., Gastown. 604-559-5180. www.brooklyngastown.com.

The latest star in a growing constellation of Gastown venues, this roomy new high-ceilinged nightclub resonates with a brick-wall warehouse vibe, as befits its location. Despite abundant tucked-away seating, a high-tech sound system drives the music into every nook and cranny.

Caprice Nightclub

967 Granville St., Downtown. 604-685-3288. capricenightclub.com.

The ever-popular Caprice is one of the city's more casual nightclubs, with couches and balconies lending it a lounge feel, though with its house, hip-hop and Top 40 tunes, and oft-heaving dance floor, there's no mistaking its real intentions.

River Rock Casino Resort

8811 River Rd., Richmond. 604-247-8900. www.riverrock.com.

The spiffy new building that houses this complex of entertainment and business venues creates an image of tradition and excitement. Inside you'll find the typical casino accoutrements, but beyond that, it's a fairly priced hotel with top-notch dining facilities, an Absolute Spa, and a convention and meeting centre. World-class stand-up comics perform on the main stage, interspersed with well-known musical acts from yesteryear and today. It's a comprehensive location for fun and business rolled into one.

MUST DO

Bacchus Lounge

Celebrities Nightclub

1022 Davie St., Downtown.
604-681-6180. www.celebrities
nightclub.com.
Recently renovated, with state-
of-the art sound, this club offers
a smorgasbord of different music,
and two floors of dancing and bars.
This all-welcoming club has been
a West End fixture for nearly 30
years, a remarkable run for such an
in-the-know nightspot.

The Charles Bar

136 W. Cordova St., Downtown
604-568-8040.
www.thecharlesbar.ca.
The Charles inhabits a triangular
footprint at the base of the
remarkable Woodward Building,
a layout that allows floods of
daylight to pour through its
generous picture windows. The
Charles does everything well,
with prompt friendly service, a
tidy but thoughtful selection of
well-executed comfort food, and a
first-class menu of micro-brews.

Fountainhead Pub

1025 Davie St. 604-687-2222.
www.thefountainheadpub.com.
Although it's famed for drawing a
discriminating clientele, and shares
its name with a weighty book, the
Fountainhead is nonetheless fun,
unpretentious and surprisingly
affordable.

Gerard Lounge

845 Burrard St., in the Sutton Place
Hotel, Downtown. 604-682-5511.
www.vancouver.suttonplace.com.
This nightspot's clubby, quiet
ambience within the luxurious
Sutton Place Hotel is legendary for
attracting film celebrities—and
you can indeed spot stars here. Its
low-key atmosphere also makes it
a comfortable space to sit and talk.

Irish Heather

210 Carrall St., Gastown. 604-688-
9779. www.irishheather.com.
This gastropub/club is a great
place to hear one of Vancouver's
most popular genres—Celtic

NIGHTLIFE

Irish Heather

music. Irish Heather features live performers most nights, including occasional appearances by well-known local bands.

900 West Lounge

900 W. Georgia St., in the Fairmont Hotel Vancouver, Downtown. 604-662-1900. www.fairmont.com/hotelvancouver.

Downtown's largest adult lounge encompasses a vast open space in the glitzy Art Moderne lobby of the venerable Hotel Vancouver. Jazz pianists and vocal artists entertain nightly, and hors-d'oeuvres and tapas are available from the hotel restaurant.

Oasis Restaurant and Bar

1240 Thurlow St., West End. 604-685-1724. www.oasis ondavie.com.

Customers here enjoy a huge selection of comfort food and cocktails in an upscale bar-lounge atmosphere, accompanied by nightly events like Slow-Dance Fridays and Sin Saturdays. The rooftop patio overlooking Davie St. is a highlight.

When the Stars Come Out

With an average of a half-dozen film productions underway at any given time in Vancouver, star-gazing is a popular pastime. The best places in the city for seeing stars are: the **Bacchus Lounge**, in the Wedgewood Hotel *(see above)*; **Gotham Steakhouse** downtown *(615 Seymour St.; 604-605-8282; www.gothamsteakhouse.com)*; **Joe Fortes Seafood & Chop House** in the West End *(777 Thurlow St.; 604-669-1940; www.joefortes.ca; see Restaurants)*; and Yaletown's **Elbow Room Cafe** *(560 Davie St.; 604-685-3628; www.theelbowroomcafe.com)* for a late breakfast.

MUST DO

Railway Club

Railway Club
579 Dunsmuir St., Downtown.
604-681-1625. www.therailway
club.com.
Lines are often long to get into this live-rock and alternative-music emporium that's been in business since 1931. And if you aren't dressed right (don't show up in your rodeo duds or three-piece suit), you might as well go someplace else.

Rain UltraClub
66 Water St., Gastown.
778-384-9878.
This bold newcomer—it opened in 2014—has injected a heady blast of Vegas-style pizzazz to the city's nightlife scene, with thumping state-of-the-art sound delivery, generous seating, and a design-heavy second-floor lounge that is perfect for people watching. Nestled into the ceiling are 20,000 lights, a bright galaxy of tiny stars that provides a vivid antidote to the dark watery weather outside.

Republic
958 Granville St. 604-669-3266.
wwwdonnellygroup.ca
Committed to music and dance, this club rocks with live music and DJs 7 nights a week, opening at 9pm and hopping until the wee hours. Fashioned after the London genre of trendy clubs, it boasts two floors of thumping rhythm, the upper one offering table service for more discriminating clientele.

Yaletown Brewing Co.
1111 Mainland St., Yaletown.
604-681-2739. www.mjg.ca/
yaletown.
Yaletown's leading sports bar is a boisterous place to be on hockey night, and before and after games at BC Place Stadium and Rogers Arena. Pub-style food here is supplemented by house-made ales, stouts and other hearty brews. It's a great place to go if you want to be part of the crowd, and a lively one at that.

NIGHTLIFE

SPAS

Yes, it does occasionally rain in Vancouver (more than 150 days a year receive some sort of precipitation), but don't wait for a rainy day to luxuriate in one of the city's elegant 🌿 spas. Most major spas in Vancouver are associated with upscale hotels, but even if you're not a guest at a particular property, you can still take advantage of its spa. Reservations are a good idea, but if your spa experience is a last-minute choice, many of the ones listed below can fit you in for some scented oils and a relaxing massage.

DAY SPAS

Absolute Spa at the Century

1015 Burrard St., at the Century Plaza Hotel. 604-684-2772. www.absolutespa.com.
Located in the lower level of the Century Plaza Hotel in mid-downtown, the Absolute pioneered the spa industry in Vancouver. Its fine reputation and established clientele combine to make it hard to get into at the last minute. If you do get in, you'll find a full menu of pampering here, from facials and manicures to mud wraps—in addition to such complementary services as light meals, eucalyptus steam, and an ozone-treated pool.

Got jet lag? Absolute has three branch operations at Vancouver International Airport (two in the terminals and one at the Fairmont Vancouver Airport Hotel). Two more locations of Absolute have opened recently, one at the River Rock Casino Resort complex in Richmond, and another at Park Royal Mall in North Vancouver. There is also an Absolute Spa at the Fairmont Hotel Vancouver *(see below)*.

The Spa at the Wedgewood Hotel

© Wedgewood Hotel & Spa

© Wickaninnish Inn

Ancient Cedars Spa

At the Wickaninnish Inn, Tofino (see Hotels). Located on the lower level of the oceanside lodge near Pacific Rim National Park Reserve, the spa at the **Wickaninnish Inn** sports a saltwater theme, utilizing thalassotherapy, seaweed wraps, sea-salt scrubs and the like to reflect the environment just out the door. The surroundings are exquisite—a leisurely hour-long walk on the long, sandy beach is the perfect way to conclude an afternoon of spa pampering.

Vida Spa, The Sutton Place Hotel Vancouver

845 Burrard St., at the Sutton Place Hotel. 604-682-8432. www.vancouver.suttonplace.com.
Yes, those Hollywood types do like to pamper themselves. Vida Spa's host hotel is Sutton Place, a huge favourite with the film industry. Vida has long experience in taking care of discriminating spa clientele who demand the most gratifying, most comprehensive and most effective body treatments. Accordingly, the spa's stone massage utilizes 54 hot stones and 18 cool ones to both relax and re-energize tired muscles. Treat yourself to the ultimate package, which combines a massage, facial, manicure, pedicure, reflexology and—ah, Hollywood—winds up with a champagne lunch.

Absolute Spa at The Fairmont Hotel Vancouver

900 W. Georgia St. 604-648-2909. www.absolutespa.com/fairmont-hotel-vancouver/.
The Fairmont's spa treatments include wraps, facials and infusions using Canadian rose-hip oil, whose healing properties are substantial. Try one of the European kur treatments, which replenish your body's lost nutrients using thermal mineral water, sea salts from France, mineral-rich moor

SPAS

Skoah

© Skoah

mud and purifying algae. If you want to work up a sweat before your massage, the facility includes fitness equipment along with saunas, a whirlpool, and swimming pools.

The Spa at the Wedgewood Hotel

845 Hornby St., at the Wedgewood Hotel. 604-608-5340. www.wedgewoodhotel.com/ spa-wedgewood/.

Vancouver's best-known boutique hotel boasts a spa that draws on the hotel's international flavour for its character.

The all-natural Epicuren line of skin products, used in facials, scrubs and other treatments, is designed to stimulate the body's immune system. Other distinctive treatments include Lavender Body Bliss, a scrub, wrap and lotion application all using lavender essence. Try the eucalyptus steam treatment after your workout in the fitness centre.

The Spa at the Wedgewood won the prestigious 2012 Consumers Choice award for best day spa in the Vancouver area. Indulge!

Skoah

1007 Hamilton St. 604-642-0200 or 888-697-5624. www.skoah.com.

The focus in this hip Yaletown spa is on skin care for the head and back. Try "sunny side down," a facial for your back with cleansing, exfoliation, detoxification and massage. The "up and down" combines facials for both head and back. Treatments here are more reasonably priced than at the big hotel spas. New locations include North Vancouver, Kitsilano, 2737 Granville St., and Metrotown.

Vida Spa

In Sheraton Vancouver Wall Centre Hotel, 1088 Burrard St. 604-331-1000; 800-401-4018 (Canada) or 888-865-2630 (USA). www.vidaspas.com.

MUST DO

Located in downtown Vancouver's largest hotel, Vida specializes in applying Ayurveda, the ancient Indian herbal wellness regime, to modern practices and techniques. Body scrubs, wraps and massages utilizing Ayurvedic essences and lotions all induce a heightened sense of health and balance. Vida Spas are also located in Vancouver's Westin Bayshore Inn and at the Fairmont Château Whistler.

DESTINATION SPAS

These spa getaways blend Canada's Western ranching tradition with wholly modern health and wellness philosophies. BC's cattle-ranching district, the Cariboo, lies four to five hours away by car from Vancouver. The treatments you will experience at these ranches are worth the drive.

🛶 Echo Valley Ranch

On Jesmond Rd., in Clinton. 404km/251mi north of Vancouver. 250-459-2386 or 800-253-8831. www.evranch.com. 20 rooms.

A New Age retreat overlooking Fraser Canyon, this ranch ranks as a North American centre for the teaching and practice of Thai massage. Here you'll don lightweight pajamas for a "work out" of stretches and limb extensions with the assistance of a skillful therapist. A hydro treatment might follow.

A day of horseback riding, a pampering massage and the lodge's Austrian-inspired cuisine all induce a sense of serenity as you watch the sun set over the Chilcotin Mountains.

The Hills Health Ranch

On Hwy. 97 in the town of 108-Mile Ranch. 487km/302mi north of Vancouver. 250-791-5225 or 800-668-2233. www.spabc.com. 46 units.

This health retreat/guest ranch draws clients from all over North America, and often on a repeat basis. They come for intensive rejuvenation and weight-loss programs here that combine exercise, recreation in the Cariboo parkland, body treatments and healthy cuisine. The ranch's signature rose-hip oil, made from rose hips actually gathered each fall in the area, is a superlative therapeutic lotion. All meals from the kitchen are prepared with nutritious ingredients designed to promote your fitness and general well being. Recreational activities include horseback riding, 🥾 **hiking and biking** on surrounding trails threading the 20,000 acres of ranch property.

Pink clay facial, The Hills Health Ranch

© The Hills Health Ranch

SPAS

RESTAURANTS

The venues listed below were selected for their ambience, location and/or value for money. Rates indicate the average cost of an appetizer, entrée and dessert for one person (not including tax, gratuity or beverages). Restaurants listed are open daily for lunch and dinner, unless otherwise noted; most accept credit cards and take online reservations. Call for information regarding reservations, dress code and opening hours. For locations of restaurants mentioned in this guide, see Restaurants in the Index.

Luxury	**$$$$** over $75	*Moderate*	**$$** $25 to $50
Expensive	**$$$** $50 to $75	*Inexpensive*	**$** less than $25

VANCOUVER

Luxury

Le Crocodile
$$$$ **French**
909 Burrard St. 604-669-4298.
www.lecrocodilerestaurant.com.
If you don't mind eating beneath the gaze of a smiling crocodile, this place will delight you. Though the room has an urban shopping-plaza sensibility (down to the parquet flooring), its white tablecloths, table lamps, and red and russet accents give the space charm. For 30 years, Le Crocodile has offered a fusion of classic French cuisine with West Coast nuances. The five-course chef's tasting menu is uber-popular, especially when paired with wines.

YEW seafood + bar
$$$$ **Contemporary**
791 W. Georgia St., in the Four Seasons Hotel. 604-692-4939.
www.yewseafood.com.
An upscale restaurant with options for lower-priced dining, Yew lets you go wild in your selections, or moderate, and still enjoy a superb meal. Its "modern coastal" menus, which change with the local fishing seasons, include vegan dinner and lunch dishes. Yew has a communal dining table, and the decor is dressed in a slick combination of warm wood and glass. Sundays deliver half-off bottled wine, a real deal. Try the luscious paella as an appetizer, followed by lobster tacos or a rich seafood stew, and topped off with an ice-cream sandwich or a selection of BC cheeses.

Expensive

🍴 Bacchus
$$$ **French**
845 Hornby St., in the Wedgewood Hotel. 604-608-5319 www.wedgewoodhotel.com. The contemporary French dishes rely heavily on West Coast ingredients. Roast rosemary-studded lamb, top-grade steak, and regional fish such as BC salmon, Haida Gwaii halibut filets, sablefish and Alaskan scallops typify the changing menu. The dessert standout, crème brûlée is presented in clever combinations like cardamom and ginger with poached pear. Luxurious upholstery, dark woods and Venetian-glass lamps above the tables help create a muted, refined atmosphere. Brunch and afternoon tea are served on weekends, and the lounge features live piano music in the evenings.

Bishop's

$$$ **West Coast**

2183 W. 4th Ave. 604-738-2025.
www.bishopsonline.com.
Dinner only.

John Bishop is widely credited with inaugurating modern fine dining in Vancouver when he opened his namesake restaurant in Kitsilano, after studying under master chef and local notable, Umberto Menghi. When he's not writing books or leading culinary tours to distant countries, Bishop himself still greets diners, and personable service distinguishes the low-key, white-tablecloth setting. The menu is a changing array of West Coast innovation, typified by eat-local entrées like BC ling cod, Fraser Valley duck, assiette of Pitt Meadows beef, and for dessert, brown butter rhubarb tart.

Blue Water Cafe + Raw Bar

$$$ **Seafood**

1095 Hamilton St. 604-688-8078.
www.bluewatercafe.net.
Dinner only.

Blue Water artfully presents wild-sourced and sustainable gourmet seafood that is exceptional. The signature dish, the appetizer tower, rises as a multilevel set of trays with about a dozen treats piled on it—prawns, oysters, seared tuna, smoked jellyfish, scallops, and salmon ceviche, to name a few. Many diners order only this dish for dinner. The raw bar offers fine sushi, and main dishes are expertly cooked fish filets, ranging from sturgeon to cod, but save room for the Cuban chocolate cake. Warm wood tones and side lighting create an elegant atmosphere in this reconfigured Yaletown warehouse.

© Le Crocodile

Le Crocodile

C Restaurant

$$$ **Seafood**

1600 Howe St. 604-681-1164.
www.crestaurant.com.

Proprietor and environmentalist Harry Kambolis was one of the first restaurant entrepreneurs to base an entire menu on local ingredients, and BC albacore tuna, Pacific octopus, line-caught ling cod, local Dungeness crab and other delicacies from nearby seas are among C's specialties. Most entrées are seared, poached or otherwise lightly cooked in the West Coast style. Options for those with more timid palates include lean flatiron steak (order it medium or less), wild salmon burger, and classic fish and chips with minted peas and tartar sauce. The minimalist black and white decor is airy (a visit to the whimsically decorated bathrooms is a must), and the patio overlooking False Creek is the best seat in the house on sunny days.

Diners in Vancouver soon become familiar with the Ocean Wise symbol, which is featured on menus and seafood displays throughout the city. Ocean Wise is a Vancouver Aquarium program that works with restaurants, markets, and suppliers to help them make ocean-friendly buying decisions. The Ocean Wise symbol is the aquarium's assurance that a particular seafood item is sustainable. See www.oceanwise.ca for more information.

Recommended by the Vancouver Aquarium as ocean-friendly.

Cioppino's Mediterranean Grill

$$$ Italian

1133 Hamilton St. 604-688-7466.
www.cioppinosyaletown.com.
Attentive service reaches its peak at this high-end Yaletown restaurant, where an array of waiters stands ready to spring into action. The open, exhibition kitchen seems impossibly busy, with a small army of cooks and waiters hustling in and out. Somehow it all works. This renovated warehouse features huge beams overhead, but the industrial feel is softened by cherry-wood trim. The "Cucina Naturale" Italian-style cuisine, low in animal fats, is exceptional, with pastas, risottos and lightly cooked local crustaceans highlighting the dinner menu. For dessert, try the tiramisu, resplendent with mascarpone, chocolate sorbet and cappuccino foam.

Diva at the Met

$$$ West Coast

645 Howe St., in the Metropolitan Hotel. 604-602-7788.
www.metropolitan.com/diva.
One of the birthplaces of Vancouver's West Coast cuisine (Diva calls it "Cascadian"), this restaurant prides itself on using ingredients traceable to local farmers, fishermen and artisanal producers. Diva features an open kitchen, some 500 wines, a five-course tasting menu and a chef's table for a singular dining experience within a setting of warm woods and subdued accents. Signature dishes include smoked black cod—gently braised—and house-cured salmon tataki; fish is dominant on the menu. Diva is especially popular for pre-theatre dinners and brunch.

Joe Fortes Seafood & Chop House

$$$ American

777 Thurlow St. 604-669-1940.
www.joefortes.ca.
Joe's specialty is raw oysters—more than a dozen kinds on most nights, affording diners an opportunity to savour the taste differences of bivalves grown in a variety of waters. Among the 50 types of fish served, the most-requested entrées are grilled or pan-seared filets of halibut, cod, salmon and rockfish. Hand-cut Canadian steaks and succulent chops round out the meaty menu. For a personalized meal, combine turf with surf at this classic West End haunt, where dark woods and a horseshoe-shaped bar lend a clubby, old-school atmosphere. In business for three decades, Joe's

has achieved legendary status. The onion rings (the best in Vancouver), along with a lengthy wine list, may be part of the reason.

LIFT

$$$ **Contemporary**

333 Menchions Mews. 604-689-5438. www.liftbarandgrill.com.
Housed in a sleek two-storey building suspended above the water near Stanley Park, this restaurant—which seems to float over Coal Harbour—has a one-of-a-kind location. Lift turns out consistently delightful urban food and serves a wide variety of wines, many of them vinted in BC. Meat-lovers will go for the terrine appetizer with quail, venison, foie gras and rabbit. The main courses span all forms of meat, poultry and fish; sushi and tempura are popular. Dishes include grilled trout with black sesame, wild mushroom ravioli, and Australian kangaroo loin with porcini and leeks, all served with seasonal local vegetables.

Miku

$$$ **Japanese**

1055 W. Hastings St. 604-568-3900. www.mikurestaurant.com.
Miku serves *aburi* sushi—flame-seared to enhance the natural flavour of the fish—and other top-end Japanese treats fused with French and Italian influences. The menu runs the creative gamut from high-style raw dishes to slow-roasted prime rib. Served in a minimalist modern interior, dishes are presented with maximum artistry. Signature desserts, such as passion-fruit praline dome and citrus ricotta strudel, are like works of art. The sweeping marble bar

creates a focal point in the sleek space. Miku is open for lunch and dinner, and has a varied wine list to complement the singular dishes.

Moderate

Adesso Bistro

$$ **Modern Italian**

1906 Haro St. (near Gilford). 604-568-9975. www.adessobistro.net. No lunch. Brunch on weekends.
This West End eatery features a modest menu filled with Italian classics, and tosses in a little contemporary spice for added flair. The word translates more or less as "in the moment," and indeed the food is served fresh as can be. Unpretentious and lively, the owners have created a homey, happy indoor-outdoor atmosphere with dependably delicious dishes. Among the house specialties is superb aragosta, a lobster and saffron risotto. Patrons rave about the pasta, and often cite the garlic-rich *linguine alle vongole* (clams) with white wine and herbs as a favourite.

Bitter

$$ **Pub Food**

16 W. Hastings St., Gastown (near Carrall). 604-558-4658. www.bitter tastingroom.com. Closed Sun.
The emphasis here on is handcrafted BC beers, and a snack-style menu that balances well with the various levels of brew bitterness. The 13 rotating taps offer a revolving selection of lagers and ales to suit every season: dark oatmeal and organic stouts for rainy winter days, light lagers for summer, and tempting pale ales and home-brewed bitters that beckon any time of year. Cocktails

and wine are available, but beer rules, and the menu that supports it ranges from all-beef chili dogs and classic scotch egg, to yummy tacos stuffed with spicy beef, local tuna, pulled pork or falafel. Try the pretzel sambo made from a fresh-baked pretzel cut in half and filled with jalapeno and Swiss cheese, ham, and roasted peppers.

Cardero's

$$ **Seafood**
1583 Coal Harbour Quay. 604-669-7666. www.carderos.com.
Perched on a pier over Coal Harbour, between downtown and Stanley Park, Cardero's is famed for "fish, chops and a wok." The up-tempo menu hews to seafood mainstays—you can't go wrong with the fish and chips, the grilled salmon is done just right, and the shrimp-topped Caesar salad does justice to both salads and seafood. Call ahead for a window table to get the best vantage point while supping tapas, grilled meat, fresh fish, pizza, pasta or, on occasion, fresh Atlantic lobster. Almost every diner is treated to a luminescent view of yachts moored at the nearby marina.

CinCin Ristorante

$$ **Italian**
1154 Robson St. 604-688-7338. www.cincin.net.
Mustard- and blood-orange-coloured stucco walls with brick trim combine to give this bustling bistro a warm and intimate Mediterranean air, a cross between a grotto and a courtyard. The cheerful wood-fired oven infuses subtle smoky flavours into the seasonal, market-driven recipes. The stylish Italian cuisine

melds traditional dishes with gourmet embellishments—classic *ossobuco alla Milanese*, pastas and risottos, pizzas and shellfish pots. Ingredients are sourced in Canada, and the kitchen offers gluten-free pizza, bread and pasta. Fare ranges from hearty—barbecue rack of Alberta lamb with spring artichokes, wood-grilled T-bone alla Florence—to lighter local offerings like wild BC halibut with crispy risotto gnocchi, or salmon flanked by baby peas, broad beans and spinach with basil pesto.

🚣 Pink Pearl

$$ **Chinese**
1132 E. Hastings St. 604-253-4316. www.pinkpearl.com.
Every morning at the crack of dawn, the dim sum cooks arrive at Pink Pearl to start preparing the day's delicacies. Every day near noon, cars and taxis start to pull up, disgorging workers from downtown who come for a dim sum lunch. By 12:30pm the vast room is packed, and the dim sum ladies are plying the aisles with baskets and plates of dumplings, rolls, cakes and stuffed pastries—vegetarian, seafood, fruit- or meat-filled; rice, wheat or taro flour; hot, sweet, sour or all three. By 2pm, the day's selection is depleted, so don't come late.

The Sandbar

$$ **Seafood**
1535 Johnson St., Granville Island. 604-669-9030. www.vancouver dine.com/sandbar.
Tucked under the dramatic steel beams of the Granville Street bridge, this cavernous 300-seat eatery is a hub of activity busy with waiters and a large kitchen staff;

Fine Dining in the Wilds of BC

Artisanal food and wine tours "in the most unlikely places" are offered by the unique tour company, Swallowtail Tours. From a one-day Vancouver-area wine tour for $39 to a three-day boutique winery tour, the budding sommelier traveller will find singular wines produced in small batches before they get snapped up by eager restaurateurs and chefs. These winery tours go in-depth, helping wine lovers make the connection between what they sip and the terroir that delivers the grapes. Among the more popular and unusual tours of BC gourmet food and wine are the crab-cooking tour that features catching, cooking and eating dungeness crab right on the beach, and the foraging tour to secret spots where you'll find (and eat!) salmonberries, wild mushrooms and Indian rhubarb. For the ultimate in BC wine and food, a special tour has party members snowshoe to a mountain top that overlooks Vancouver for a three-course meal served in the snow. All tours are guided. www.swallowtail.ca.

the mood is upbeat and lively. The specialty is fresh fish: lobster, crab and mussels are drawn directly from a tank of live shellfish and cooked a-la-minute. Some items have an Asian heritage: coconut prawns, pad Thai, ginger beef, coconut jasmine rice, and sushi *(served daily 5:30pm–10:30pm)* jostle for menu space along with traditional favourites like cedar-planked West Coast salmon, a Sandbar specialty. For diners who can't decide, prawns, lobster or crab can be added to a top-quality steak that's grilled to perfection. Live music in the lounge seven days a week *(8:30pm–11:30pm)*.

Sawasdee
$$ **Thai**
4250 Main St. 604-876-4030.
www.sawasdeethairestaurant.com.
Vancouver's first authentic Thai restaurant still excels at blending BC ingredients with Thai flavours and techniques. Red coconut-milk curries are a house specialty, and the roasted duck curry is exceptional, as is the chicken-breast curry with young coconut meat. Many diners consider

Sawasdee's pad Thai to be the city's best. Patrons are given the option to order their meals from mild to very hot, and are invariably thrilled with the presentations, often graced with flowers (mostly edible). The softly lit stucco interior lends a tropical air, and the unpretentious family-owned ambiance puts diners at ease.

Shabusen Yakiniku House
$$ **Japanese/Korean**
755 Burrard St. (at 14th Ave). 604-669-3883. www.shabusen.com.
This Japanese-Korean sushi-barbecue eatery is hopping at lunchtime, so arrive early or make reservations. You can order from the menu, but most in the know choose the buffet, and use the BBQ grill in the middle of the tables to cook their selections. For lighter fare—or as appetizers for a full meal—the sushi menu is among the best in town. Shabusen specialises in Japanese "Yakiniku" cuisine, so expect plenty of barbecued meat dipped in delicious soy-infused sauces flavoured with garlic, miso, sake, and sesame.

Sun Sui Wah Seafood Restaurant

$$ **Cantonese**
3888 Main St. 604-872-8822.
www.sunsuiwah.com

Given the atmosphere – aquarium-sized tanks brimming with live seafood, dim sum trolleys rolling through the aisles, the cheerful din of happy diners, and the succulent house specialty of roasted squab – diners could be forgiven for thinking they had somehow ended up in Hong Kong. Sun Sui Wah does have its roots in the Hong Kong suburb of Shatin, but a closer look at the menu—or at the tanks—reveals West Coast specialties like Alaska king crab, geoduck, Dungeness crab, and halibut, and the resulting fusion generates some of the finest Cantonese food in the city. Don't miss the steamed king crab with garlic, or the flash-fried geoduck, and if you've never tried roast pigeon before, this is the place to do it.

🍴 Vij's

$$ **Indian**
1480 W. 11th Ave. 604-736-6664.
www.vijsrestaurant.ca. Dinner only.

Patrons make pilgrimages here from across Canada to experience Vikram Vij's edgy Indian cuisine. The no-reservations policy means dinner hopefuls line up early, by 5pm for the 5:30pm opening, and wait patiently to experience the lovely, aromatic atmosphere. What's the draw? The culinary inventions, such as BC trout in coconut and fenugreek masala with wheat berry pilaf; braised beef ribs with roasted okra, walnuts and jelly beans; or wine-marinated lamb "popsicles" in cream curry, created by the all-female Punjabi kitchen staff.

Inexpensive

Meat & Bread

$ **Sandwiches**
370 Cambie St. and 1033 West Pender St. www.meatandbread.ca. Lunch only.

This is the sandwich as it was first conceived: stripped to its essentials, free of sloppy dressings and multiple bread choices, and with meticulous emphasis on a few simple ingredients. Fresh ciabatta is the only bread available, and condiments are limited to a touch of mustard or a hint of sambal. The porchetta sandwich, made from thick fat rolls of herb-flavoured free-range grain-fed pork, is the signature filling, and spicy meatballs, a daily roast, and a cheese option for vegetarians round out the menu.

Phnom Penh

$ **Pan-Asian**
244 E. Georgia St. 604-682-5777.

This Chinatown institution takes Asian comfort food to a whole new level, as the churning kitchen delivers a steady stream of reliably delicious dishes, in the loud, happy, "hot and noisy" atmosphere that typifies the best family restaurants in Asia. Efficient, no-nonsense staff navigate the busy tables and dispense helpful menu advice. Black pepper squid is a highlight, and deep-fried chicken wings are a house specialty, but the huge menu features a pan-Asian cornucopia of shrimp salad rolls, stir-fried *gai lan* and *bok choy*, steamed locally caught fish, spicy basil clams, papaya salad, hot heaping platters of noodles and fried rice, and many more. Reservations are a must.

Holds summary for Gruenhut, Allen H.
Sat Aug 19 11:26:12 EDT 2017

#: 1
BARCODE: 31489006632200
CALL NUM: 917.1133 S 2015
LOCATION: frl00
TITLE: Frommer's easyguide to Vancouver
PICKUP AT: EAST MEADOW
NOT AFTER: 02-09-2018 1:11PM
STATUS: AVAILABLE

#: 2
BARCODE: 31736006276853
CALL NUM: 917.1133 F 5th Ed 2017
LOCATION: fal00
TITLE: Vancouver & Victoria.
PICKUP AT: EAST MEADOW
NOT AFTER: 02-09-2018 1:14PM
STATUS: 08-21-2017

East Meadow Public Library

1886 Front Street ◦ East Meadow, NY 11554
516.794.2570 ◦ 516.794.2949 (TTY)
www.eastmeadow.info

Stepho's Souvlaki Greek Taverna

$ **Greek**

1124 Davie St. 604-683-2555.
Sometimes the line to get into
Stepho's stretches out the door,
down the street and around the
corner at lunch and dinner. All those
people come for heaping platters
of Greek roast lamb, potatoes, salad
and vegetables—an utterly filling,
yet economical meal that will last
all day. Yes, they have baklava, but
it's hard to find the room for it after
finishing off a dinner platter.

Vera's Burger Shack

$ **American**

1181 Denman St. 604-681-5450.
www.verasburgershack.com
Vancouver burger-lovers know they
can count on one of the many Vera's
locations for their fix—and hungry
kids craving something "normal" will
leave satisfied without breaking the
bank, while adults can complement
their burgers with a draft beer.
Established as a beach concession
in 1977, the fast-growing chain
offers poutine, homemade chili,
thick creamy milkshakes, and other
diner-style delights to flesh out
its menu of chicken, lamb, turkey,
veggie and beef burgers.

VANCOUVER ISLAND

Luxury

🏠 Sooke Harbour House

$$$$ **West Coast**

Whiffen Spit Rd., Sooke. 250-642-
3421. www.sookeharbourhouse.
com. Closed Tue. and Wed.
When Sinclair and Frederique
Philip opened a small inn in the
mid-1970s to offer New Wave
cuisine based on local ingredients,

few other cooks in Canada were
exploring those frontiers. Today an
entire cuisine (West Coast) borrows
their pioneering principles, and
gourmands fly across the continent
to have dinner here. What they
find every night is different, but
the menu always draws on local
seafood (such as oysters, sea
cucumbers, rockfish and 10 kinds
of seaweed), artisanal cheeses,
fresh vegetables, and herbs and
berries grown in the inn's gardens.

Expensive

Bengal Lounge

$$$ **Indian**

721 Government St., in the Empress
Hotel, Victoria. 250-384-8111.
www.fairmont.com/empress-
victoria/dining/thebengallounge.
The Empress Hotel's less-formal
dining room is redolent with Empire
decor—polished mahogany, ceiling
fans, potted palms, red-leather
armchairs, even a tiger skin on the
wall. The lounge dates back to the
1950s, and is noted for its inventive
array of martinis and tropical drinks.
At lunch and dinner, a long table is
laden with ingredients for the curry
buffet, ranging from coconut-
chicken to mango chutney, while
the à la carte menu features pub
classics like pulled pork sandwiches,
seafood chowder, and halibut and
chips. The Bengal Lounge features
live music most evenings *(Thu–Sun)*.

Café Brio

$$$ **Italian**

944 Fort St., Victoria. 250-383-
0009. www.cafe-brio.com.
Dinner only.
A decade after pioneering bistro
cuisine in Victoria, Café Brio finds its
popularity unabated. The intriguing

decor (Modigliani-style nudes on the walls, unadorned fir-plank floors, 18-feet ceilings) serves as a backdrop for home-style Italian cooking featuring light flavourings and regional ingredients. Pan-fried local seafoods, wine-braised short ribs, and homemade smoked and cured meats accentuate the menu, while the signature pasta dishes and tempting desserts are not to be missed.

ulla

$$$　　　**Contemporary**
509 Fisgard St., Victoria. 250-590-8795. www.ulla.ca. Dinner only.
Located on the edge of Victoria's Chinatown, ulla is dressed up in warehouse chic, with high ceilings, arched windows, brick interiors and unadorned fir tables that create a cosy art-gallery atmosphere. Diners who can overlook the curt service – and they should – will be rewarded with a cuisine that is fresh and inventive, with each dish delivering its own individual suite of spice-and-texture pleasures. The small but carefully selected menu tends toward the meaty end of the dining spectrum, but vegetarians and seafood-eaters

are not ignored: the grilled tofu and tempeh entrée, surrounded by a crunchy sea of herbs, nuts and vegetables, is creative and unusual.

Moderate

Ming's

$$　　　**Chinese**
1321 Quadra St., Victoria. 250-385-4405. www.mings.ca. Dinner only.
Though it occasionally ventures into Szechuan or Hunan cuisine, Ming's specializes in classic Cantonese dishes in Victoria's Chinatown. After entering the dining room through an ivory moon gate, you'll experience service that is infinitely attentive. All the southern Chinese classics are on the menu, from egg rolls and sauteed seasonal vegetables to sweet-and-sour pork and salt-and-pepper calamari. The restaurant offers delivery service daily from 4:30pm.

🍴 Spinnaker's Gastro Brewpub

$$　　　**Pub Food**
308 Catherine St., Victoria. 250-386-2739. www.spinnakers.com.
Spinnaker's claims to be the first licenced brewpub in Canada—a distinction it enhances considerably with this restaurant perched beside the Inner Harbour. Dining fare is upscale pub food, such as a tasting plate of island artisan cheeses, a braised-lamb sandwich, and yeast-battered fish and chips. The huge menu is laden with pastas, pies, oysters, burgers, nachos, sandwiches, desserts and more; try a piping hot thin-crust pizza direct from the wood oven, topped off with home-made ice cream or chevre cheesecake for

ulla

© Brent Hannon / Michelin

dessert. The brews are highly flavoured, and very fresh. Breakfast is also served.

Inexpensive

Blue Fox Cafe
$ **American**
919 Fort St., Victoria. 250-380-1683. www.thebluefoxcafe.com. Breakfast and Lunch only.
It's easy to find the Blue Fox: just look for the queue out on the sidewalk, especially for weekend breakfasts or weekday lunches. The fare here is not exotic—breakfast platters piled high with hotcakes, thick toast, fat omelettes and sausages, and the locally famous eggs Benedict. Lunch means big handmade hamburgers and hand-cut fries and meatloaf. Breakfast is served all day, if your patience is tested by the morning lines. Because Blue Fox is so busy, don't expect to be in and out in half an hour.

Common Loaf Bake Shop
$ **American**
180 First St., Tofino. 250-725-3915.
The loaves at this counterculture hangout in Tofino (but visitors of all persuasions are drawn here) are far from common—the thick and nutty multi-grain concoctions are a meal in themselves. There's also excellent coffee, and luscious pastries, muffins and scones in the morning from the bakery side of the cafe. At lunch and dinner *(the latter served until 6pm in winter and 7pm in summer)*, simple soups and salads are offered. The cedar-and-fir panelled interior is pure New Age, and the bulletin board is the place to find out what's happening in the West Coast alternative community.

WHISTLER

Luxury

🛁 Rimrock Cafe
$$$$ **Contemporary**
2117 Whistler Rd., Creekside (just outside Whistler) 877-932-5589. www.rimrockcafe.com. Dinner only.
"Cafe" is something of a misnomer here at Whistler's favourite fine-dining establishment. Loved by locals as the special spot for celebrations, the Rimrock has an extensive menu featuring fish and game. Popular since it opened in 1987, the restaurant makes up for a limited culinary imagination with consistency, atmosphere, and excellent service. With two fireplaces, a patio and rustic decor, Rimrock exudes a warm sensibility and oozes comfort.

elements urban tapas parlour
$$ **Tapas**
4359 Main St. (in the Summit Lodge). 604-932-5569. www.elementswhistler.com.
Just when you thought "BC" meant "bring cash," a restaurant comes along that encourages you to sup on as little or as much as you wish. Elements delivers the best of eggs Benedict in the morning, and a substantial range of tapas options for an eclectic dinner collection. The casual decor suggests intimacy and laid-back dining, a suitable backdrop to the ever-changing tapas menu. If you like beef, you'll love the perfectly prepared bison petit tender three ways. If you're vegetarian, there's plenty to choose from, too. The restaurant is owned by the people who own Whistler's well-regarded **Pacific Bistro**. *(www.wildwoodrestaurants.ca).*

HOTELS

The properties listed below were selected for their ambience, location and/or value for money. Prices (in Canadian Dollars) reflect the average cost for a standard double room for two people (not including applicable sales and hotel taxes that add 16.3% to the total cost). Hotels in Vancouver frequently offer discounts, so it's best to check online. Properties are in Vancouver, unless otherwise specified.

Luxury	**$$$$$ over $350**	*Inexpensive*	**$$ $100 to $175**
Expensive	**$$$$ $250 to $350**	*Budget*	**$ less than $100**
Moderate	**$$$ $175 to $250**		

VANCOUVER

Luxury

Fairmont Waterfront
$$$$$ 489 rooms
900 Canada Place. 604-691-1991 or 866-540-4509. www.fairmont. com/waterfront-vancouver.
The Waterfront is the Fairmont chain's downtown business hotel, a gleaming steel-and-glass tower in which every room has an expansive view—60 percent of the rooms overlook Burrard Inlet, Stanley Park and the North Shore. The rooms feature soft natural tones of sand, cream and blue, backdropped by sweeping views of the North Shore. The hotel offers guided morning runs, a walkable roof-top herb garden, and for Fairmont Gold members, free valet parking, a private concierge, and breakfast and canapés in the evening. An extensive health club, business centre, shopping arcade and ARC Restaurant and Bar round out the facilities. Canada Place sits across the street.

Four Seasons
$$$$$ 373 rooms
791 W. Georgia St. 604-689-9333 or 866-223-9333. www.fourseasons. com/vancouver.
Attentive service is the hallmark at this property, one of Vancouver's consistently top-rated hotels—if a doorman sees you returning from a jog, he'll hand you a towel and water bottle. Though not

Lobby, Fairmont Waterfront

© Fairmont Hotels & Resorts

Executive suite, Opus Hotel

overly large, the guest rooms are elegantly furnished, with brass trim, natural tones and marble baths. Hotel facilities are lavish, including an indoor-outdoor pool that opens out onto a huge second-storey garden terrace. The hotel boasts 24-hour multi-lingual concierge services and business centre, and claims to offer 300 wines by the glass!

Opus Hotel
$$$$$ 97 rooms
322 Davie St. 604-642-6787 or 866-642-6787. www.opushotel.com.
Designers of this distinctive hotel in Yaletown chose unusual decorative elements to echo the property's hip neighbourhood. Candles and settees are the lobby furnishings, and headset-adorned staffers greet guests at reception podiums. Rooms feature strong colours such as purple and ebony, and bathrooms have floor-to-ceiling windows, and a counter made from a long stone slab. Rated among the top five trendy hotels in the world, this hotel is aimed directly at hipsters.

Fairmont Hotel Vancouver
$$$$ 557 rooms
900 W. Georgia St. 604-684-3131 or 866-540-4452. www.fairmont.com/hotel-vancouver.
The Hotel Van is a Canadian icon, one of the string of château-style landmark hotels spread across the country and built near its railroads about 100 years ago. Steep gables and copper roofs characterize the familiar Vancouver landmark. Rooms often contain unaltered historic elements such as tiled baths with deep soaking tubs. Every service imaginable is on-site, including a lavish health club with a glass-roofed pool and an Absolute Spa *(see SPAS)*. The hotel is pet-friendly and even has canine concierges.

Sutton Place Hotel
$$$$ 379 rooms
845 Burrard St. 604-682-5511 or 866-378-8866. www.vancouver.suttonplace.com.
Waiting limousines line the driveway of this pink-toned palace on Burrard, which remains the film industry's favourite place to stay in Vancouver. Snazzy guest rooms have huge picture windows, ivory

and beige decor and marble baths in a classic luxury style. The service is expert and unquestioning, and every amenity imaginable is offered, from an extensive fitness facility to 24-hour room service. The adjacent La Grande Residence is a 164-unit short-term luxury apartment complex.

🛁 Wedgewood Hotel & Spa

$$$$ **83 rooms**
845 Hornby St. 604-689-7777 or 800-663-0666. www.wedgewood hotel.com.

Loyal fans of this discreet boutique hotel consider it one of Vancouver's best. Owner Eleni Skalbania chose distinctive French and Italian decor for the spacious suites, outfitted with brocade-covered couches, in-room host bars and balconies overlooking the Law Courts. The service is attentive, and a spa complements the compact health club *(see Spas)*. Bacchus restaurant *(see Restaurants)* and lounge are on the ground floor. The Vancouver Art Gallery and Robson Street

Wedgewood Hotel & Spa

© Wedgewood Hotel & Spa

shopping are just minutes away. This property is a designated Relais & Châteaux hotel, but remains a family-run business.

Moderate

Executive Hotel LeSoleil

$$$ **106 rooms**
567 Hornby St. 604-632-3000 or 877-632-3030. www.hotel lesoleil.com.

The Old-World elegance of the lobby sets the tone at this lush downtown all-suite boutique hotel—voted in the top 25 luxury hotels in Canada by a much-used travel website. The cosy rooms continue this theme, with down-pillowed beds, Biedermeier-style furniture, brocade fabrics in gold and crimson, and hushed lighting. Its downtown location is close to Canada Place, Stanley Park, the Art Gallery and Gastown, and in the heart of the shopping, financial and business districts.

Granville Island Hotel

$$$ **85 rooms**
1253 Johnston St. 604-683-7373 or 800-663-1840. www.granville islandhotel.com.

The white siding of this two-storey property evokes the many sails that float past Granville Island. The interior is contemporary, with spacious rooms furnished in soothing neutrals. The hotel faces False Creek, and sits at the quiet end of its namesake island, where cafes, stalls and galleries are just minutes away. Amenities include a full health club, restaurant and bar, and three executive suites. Pets are welcome for a modest fee, and **The Dockside Restaurant ($$)** offers a Jazz and Blues brunch.

Sortino suite, Listel Hotel

© Listel Hotel

Listel Vancouver

$$$ 129 rooms

*1300 Robson St. 604-684-8461
or 800-663-5491. www.thelistel
hotel.com.*

Local art is the distinguishing
element at this chic boutique
hotel on Robson Street. Rooms on
gallery floors are decorated with
works from the hotel's alliance
with a nearby upscale art dealer;
one floor features First Nations art
derived from an affiliation with the
UBC Museum of Anthropology *(see
Museums)*. Spacious suites have
Berber carpet, beige and maroon
hues, and cosy window seats. The
location is ideal for visiting Stanley
Park and the Vancouver Art Gallery,
and for watching the bustling
scene on Robson. The hotel boasts
a zero-waste policy, all smoke-
free rooms and facilities, and
complimentary wine receptions.

Pan Pacific

$$$ 503 rooms

*999 Canada Place. 604-662-8111
or 877-324-4856. www.panpacific.
com/vancouver.*

Perched on the shoreward end
of the Canada Place pier, the Pan
Pacific's white-sided tower faces
water on three sides, so virtually all
the rooms have expansive views
of Burrard Inlet. Asian flair flavours
the famously attentive service,
which relies on a small army of
staffers to meet guest needs. The
neutrally decorated rooms are
compact but luxuriously outfitted,
with mahogany and marble
touches. The hotel has direct
access to the Vancouver World
Trade Centre, and prime
shopping areas.

St. Regis

$$$ 72 rooms

*602 Dunsmuir St. 604-681-1135
or 800-770-7929. www.stregis
hotel.com.*

There's nothing fancy about the St.
Regis, which opened in 1913. The
rooms are compact, quiet and air-
conditioned, furnished in muted
gray tones, and are affordable
and convenient. The venerable
property has a mid-downtown
location close to Canada Place,
Gastown and Chinatown, and it
offers business centre, Internet
access (Wi-Fi), global long-distance
phone calls, a full breakfast, and
a sports club free of charge, but it
has no on-site parking.

HOTELS

St. Regis

© St. Regis

Residences on Georgia and the Palisades

$$$ **493 rooms**

1288 W. Georgia St. 604-891-6101. www.respal.com.

These sleek modern apartments are an ideal choice for longer-stay visitors to Vancouver. Furnished in muted gray, white, beige and brushed-metal trim, with small kitchenettes, breakfast nooks and small office spaces, they appeal to film-industry workers in town for shoots. Included are a screening room downstairs, access to a health club across the street, gated underground parking and private-access security. Weekly and monthly room rates compare favourably to moderate hotel rates.

Thistledown House

$$$ **5 rooms**

3910 Capilano Rd., North Vancouver. 604-986-7173 or 888-633-7173. www.thistle-down.com.

Venerable apple trees shade the backyard patio of this restored timber tycoon's North Shore mansion. The genteel 1920s Arts and Crafts-style house features stunning built-in cabinetry, especially in the formal dining

room where guests enjoy sumptuous breakfasts of house-made pastries and preserves, omelettes or French toast. Guest rooms have eclectic furnishings such as walnut four-poster beds, and the honeymoon suite boasts a heated bathroom floor and a sitting room with fireplace.

Inexpensive

The Burrard Hotel

$$ **72 rooms**

1100 Burrard St. 604-681-9753. www.theburrard.com .

The venerable Burrard has provided comfortable, reasonably priced rooms to Vancouver visitors since the days of finned Cadillacs and soda fountains – 1956, to be exact – and it plays the same role today, albeit with touches that Elvis would not have recognized, such as flatscreen TVs, MP3 docks, in-room safes, and espresso machines, courtesy of a recent renovation. Formerly a motor hotel and still an icon, the Burrard, with its vintage 1950s aura, is a refreshing throwback in a city increasingly filled with design-heavy hotels.

North Vancouver Hotel

$$ **72 rooms**

1800 Capilano Rd., North Vancouver. 604-987-4461 or 800-663-4055. www.north vancouverhotel.ca.

This colourful stucco property is a top-notch motel with an excellent location. Spacious rooms, done in pastel fabrics, are situated in quiet buildings set back from the road. A palm-bordered swimming pool, free local calls, complimentary passes to a fitness club, on-site laundry facilities and a full hot breakfast round out the amenities. The setting is ideal for visiting Grouse Mountain, and lies within a half hour of the Horseshoe Bay ferry terminal. Pets are welcome in designated rooms for a surcharge.

🛁 Sylvia Hotel

$$ **120 rooms**

1154 Gilford St. 604-681-9321 or 877-681-9321. www.sylviahotel.com.

Many is the family whose Sylvia loyalty spans generations. It is by far the best reasonably-priced hotel in downtown Vancouver, and it's close to Stanley Park to boot (with parking included).

The rooms and suites are like mid-20C apartments, with polyglot furnishings, little discernible decor scheme, ample closets and sitting rooms. Many have kitchenettes— real ones, with refrigerators, stoves, sinks and counter space. The ivy-covered brick building is a World War I-era landmark, erected in 1912 as an apartment building, facing English Bay and the seawall pedestrian path. Pets are welcome.

Budget

Hostelling International

$ **282 rooms**

1025 Granville St. (Central); 604-685-5335 or 866-762-4122; 226 rooms. 1114 Burnaby St. (Downtown); 604-684-4565 or 866-762-4122; 223 rooms. 1515 Discovery St. (Jericho Beach); 604-224-3208 or 866-762-4122. www.hihostels.ca.

All three of Vancouver's hostels offer excellent locations. Rooms (both dorm-style and private) are clean and updated. Full facilities range from media rooms to laundries and cafes, as well as staff information services. The

Sylvia Hotel

© Sylvia Hotel

HOTELS

Burrard Hotel

© The Burrard Hotel

VANCOUVER ISLAND AND WHISTLER

Luxury

The Fairmont Chateau Whistler

$$$$$　　**550 rooms**

4599 Chateau Blvd., Whistler. 604-938-8000. 800-606-8244. www.fairmont.com/whistler.

Though this hotel is one of the most upscale accommodations in Whistler, the ambience is not all palatial. The building itself, at the foot of Blackcomb Mountain, is indeed chateau-like, and the lobby, common areas and Wildflower restaurant are all refined and elegant. But the rooms, some outfitted in upscale country wood furniture and others in a neutral Neo-classical design, are relaxed and spacious—and virtually all have a view of snowcapped peaks. The proximity of the lifts means the Chateau is a ski-in, ski-out property. With a spa and golf course, this property offers complete R&R bliss.

Wickaninnish Inn

$$$$$　　**75 rooms**

500 Osprey Lane, Chesterman Beach, 2mi south of Tofino. 250-725-3100 or 800-333-4604. www.wickinn.com.

When Tofino native Charles McDiarmid opened this lodge in the early 1990s, he had a radical idea: the West Coast shore could be as appealing a destination in winter as in summer. So he designed the stone-and-timber main building with huge, sturdy plate-glass windows facing the ocean, and positioned the rooms so that the winter tempests could

downtown location is on a quiet street near Stanley Park, and the central location is handy to Granville Island, Gastown and the city's entertainment district. The Jericho Beach hostel is closest to Kitsilano and the University of British Columbia.

YWCA Hotel/Residence

$　　**155 rooms**

733 Beatty St. 604-895-5830 or 800-663-1424. www.ywcahotel.com.

A wide variety of rooms is available in this pleasant facility in the east end of downtown, from dorm-style to small kitchenette family suites. Rooms are decorated in pastels with light-coloured wood trim. A laundry, coffee shop, parking and in-room refrigerators round out the facilities; weekly and monthly rates are available. The location is close to Chinatown and the city's stadium district. Of course, the exercise facilities here are extensive.

MUST STAY

be seen while visitors enjoyed the comforts of firelight and cosy beds. Most rooms at the Wick feature balconies facing the water; many have soaking tubs, and the style is distinctly coastal in tone and accents.

Expensive

🛴 The Fairmont Empress
$$$$ **477 rooms**
721 Government St., Victoria.
250-384-8111 or 866-540-4429.
www.fairmont.com/empress.
Rooms in this landmark hotel *(see Excursions)* are as elegant as the building they occupy, with late Victorian and Neo-classical furnishings of walnut and brocade, spacious dimensions and every modern amenity; each room boasts a sitting area. Resplendent with fine dining, high tea *(booking in advance is highly recommended; a dress code is in place)* and a Willow Stream Spa, the Empress is the very definition of decorum. Every Victoria visitor should stay at the Empress at least once. The higher floors are more desirable, as nearby Government Street is the city's main thoroughfare, and a busy one. There's a premium on rooms facing the Inner Harbour, so you might get a better room at a more reasonable rate on the back side of the hotel.

Haterleigh Heritage Inn
$$$$ **6 rooms**
243 Kingston St., Victoria.
250-384-9995 or 866-234-2244.
www.haterleigh.com.
The stained-glass windows in this lavish 1901 Victorian house let light pour into the lobby, awash with crystal-and-brass decorations.

Most of the guest rooms have whirlpool tubs, and are furnished with Victorian antiques, and patterned fabrics and wallpaper in keeping with the period. Breakfasts are hearty British-style affairs, with eggs, scones, pastries and sausage. Guests enjoy complimentary afternoon tea and evening sherry.

🛴 Magnolia Hotel & Spa
$$$$ **64 rooms**
623 Courtney St., Victoria.
250-381-0999 or 877-624-6654.
www.magnoliahotel.com.
Opulence rules at this Old World-style boutique hotel. Mahogany walls, alabaster chandeliers and a gold gilt ceiling greet visitors in the compact lobby. All the rooms and suites are spacious, with floor-to-ceiling windows that let in ample light to complement the cream-and-beige decor. Large bathrooms have separate walk-in showers and soaking tubs. A long list of amenities ranges from a wet bar and fridge in every room to a full-service day spa in the hotel. The **Catalano Restaurant and Cicchetti Bar ($$$)** complements the mature elegance of the hotel. The location is ideal for walking to Fort Street, Old Town, Chinatown and the Inner Harbour.

Moderate

Bedford Regency
$$$ **40 rooms**
1140 Government St., Victoria.
250-384-6835 or 800-665-6500.
www.bedfordregency.com.
Located a short walk away from the Inner Harbour and Government Street shops, this boutique hotel has handsomely appointed guest rooms with

wood-burning fireplaces, large cushy chairs and goose-down duvets. Some rooms feature whirlpool tubs, flower-bedecked window boxes and views of James Bay. Pub fare is served on the premises in the English-style **Garrick's Head ($$)**.

Fairholme Manor
$$$ 6 suites
638 Rockland Place, Victoria. 250-598-3240 or 877-511-3322. www.fairholmemanor.com.
This stately Italianate mansion occupies a serene, large lot atop Rockland Hill, next to Government House. The 110-year-old manor comprises 7,000sq ft; the two suites in the main house boast high ceilings, bay windows overlooking the garden, and expansive baths with deep tubs. Breakfast is European, but not continental—multiple courses include eggs and pastries. All rooms are suites, decorated in an understated Victorian-era manner,

Fairholme Manor

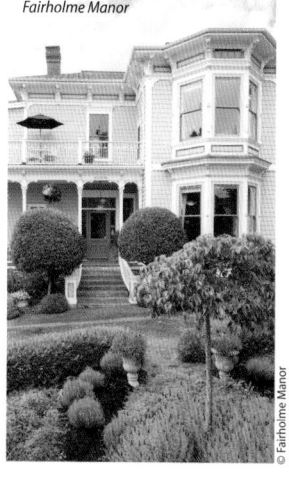

© Fairholme Manor

and with gas or wood-burning fireplaces and soaker tubs.

Listel Hotel Whistler
$$$ 98 rooms,
4121 Village Green. 604-932-1133 or 800-663-5472. www.listelhotel.com.
Located in the heart of Whistler Village, this modern, 3-storey hotel has plenty of ambience, and amenities such as a whirlpool, sauna, and an on-site restaurant open for après-ski as well as dinner. Rooms and suites offer free Internet, cable TV and in-room recycling. A continental breakfast is included in the rate.

🏖 Long Beach Lodge Resort
$$$ 41 rooms,
**   10 cottages**
1441 Pacific Rim Hwy., Tofino. 250-725-2442 or 877-844-7873. www.longbeachlodgeresort.com.
Warm, comfortable tones of wood dominate both the decor and the atmosphere at this beachfront lodge in Tofino. The lobby and public spaces feature huge Douglas-fir beams and trim, and the exterior is cedar shake, with metal roofing and stone accents. A cheery fire crackles in the large stone fireplace indoors. Rooms are done up in handmade fir furniture, with sizable soaking tubs and balconies or patios overlooking the ocean. The lodge lies steps away from a mile-long broad sand beach, with enticing headlands at either end. Pet-friendly, the lodge provides a BBQ shelter where guests can create their own meals, an outdoor hot tub, a sauna and exercise room, and offers surfing instruction and rentals.

Rosewood Victoria Inn
$$$ **17 rooms**
595 Michigan St., Victoria.
250-384-6644 or 866-986-2222.
www.viresorts.com/resorts/
Rosewood.html.

The sunny yellow exterior of this small inn near the Parliament Buildings hints at the cosy warmth inside. The airy courtyard lets in light, and the cheery wallpaper and floral fabrics in the rooms continue the Victorian and Colonial theme. Each individually decorated room has a balcony or patio; most have fireplaces. Rates include breakfast in the conservatory or outside on the heated patio.

Summit Lodge
$$$ **81 rooms**
4359 Main St., Whistler.
604-932-2778 or 888-913-8811.
www.summitlodge.com.

This low-key, expertly run boutique hotel is ideal for travellers who want to focus on the skiing and golf they came to Whistler to enjoy. The comfortable rooms have compact kitchenettes, country pine furniture and balconies; most

rooms offer stunning mountain views. The service is friendly and knowledgeable, and the location in the middle of Whistler Village is handy to on-mountain activities and village life. A pool, hot tub, sauna and spa are on the premises.

Inexpensive

Whistler Hostel International
$ **30 rooms**
1035 Legacy Way, Whistler.
604-962-0025. www.hihostels.ca.

Located 8km south of Whistler Village, this hostel was purpose-built as part of the 2010 Olympics athletes' village. It offers 108 beds in shared quarters, and 20 private rooms to members and nonmembers alike. Guest amenities include a large guest kitchen and dining room, outdoor decks with views of the surrounding mountains, a media room with a fireplace and 52-inch high-definition television, a billiards room, a sauna, and plenty of room for bicycle, ski and snowboard storage. Grab a quick meal at **Cheaky's Café ($)** and enjoy dining on the patio.

HOTELS

153

VANCOUVER

INDEX

List of Maps

INDEX